Stuart Hillard is one of the UK's leading quilt
designers, teachers and home decor experts
with over 20 years of experience and hundreds
of published patterns to his name. Known as
the star of the first series of The Great British
Sewing Bee, Stuart has authored *Sew Fabulous*;
Use Scraps, Sew Blocks, Make 100 Quilts and
Simple Shapes, Stunning Quilts. He is a regular
guest presenter on Create and Craft TV, has
appeared alongside Kirstie Allsop on Channel 4
and is a regular on BBC radio.
He writes for *Sew, Crafts Beautiful* and *Let's
Get Crafting* magazines. He is a fabric designer
and is on the judging panel for The British Craft
Business Awards, The British Sewing Awards
and Dressmaker of the Year Competition
annually. When he isn't knitting, sewing or
cooking, Stuart is likely to be found on the
88-acre farm in North Yorkshire that he and
his husband Charlie are renovating.

STUART HILLARD

BAGS FOR LIFE

21 projects to make, customise & love forever

STUART HILLARD

BAGS FOR LIFE

21 projects to make, customise & love forever

PAVILION

For Charlie... I am the fabric but you are the thread.

First published in the United Kingdom in 2021 by
Pavilion
An imprint of HarperCollins*Publishers*
1 London Bridge Street
London SE1 9GF

www.harpercollins.co.uk

HarperCollins*Publishers*
Macken House,
39/40 Mayor Street Upper,
Dublin 1
D01 C9W8
Ireland

ISBN 978-1-911663-40-9

A CIP catalogue record for this book is available
from the British Library.
10 9 8 7 6 5 4 3

Reproduction by Rival Colour, UK
Printed and bound in China by RR Donnelley APS

Illustrations: Kuo Chen
Photographer: Rachel Whiting
Publisher: Helen Lewis
Project editor: Sophie Allen
Design manager: Alice Kennedy-Owen
Production manager: Phil Brown

MIX
Paper | Supporting
responsible forestry
FSC™ C007454
FSC
www.fsc.org

CONTENTS

INTRODUCTION

Sewing is my biggest passion and my greatest pleasure, it's something I've done since I was a tot. I learned the basics of sewing before I learned to read, it was my mum's way of keeping me occupied and happy but I don't think she imagined it would sustain my whole life! Over the years I've sewn just about everything from curtains to quilts, waistcoats to wedding hats. Bags have a very special place in my heart – they are useful and practical and a very stylish way to accessorize an outfit. Anyone who knows me knows that I love bags and I'm rarely seen without one! Where else would I stash my snacks?

Seriously though, who doesn't love a bag? I've been making bags for myself and friends for many years and the reason I started was to fill a rather glaring gap. More than 20 years ago I was a member of a quilting group and we, like every sewing group I've ever visited, had a resident 'bag lady'. Ours was called Viv! She would come to class every month with another fabulous bag creation and everyone in the group would admire her work. The problem was, all the bags she made were most definitely designed for women. I asked Viv if she had any patterns suitable for men. She shook her head... perhaps, she suggested, I could create my own?

I designed my first pattern that week, a variation on the everyday messenger bag you'll find in this book, and I've been making it ever since, as well as teaching others to make bags. My designs are for everyone, regardless of gender or style. They can be made to look very simple, pared back and modern or loud, flamboyant and bursting with exuberance. Pick your bag, choose your fabrics and make it your way!

This book is for anyone who already loves making bags or has ever thought they'd like to have a go. There are designs for complete beginners right through to more advanced bag making, but at my core, I like to design projects that are achievable. None of the bags in this book require a great deal of experience – or time for that matter – so there are plenty of 'quick fix' projects for when you need to scratch that creative itch.

I've divided the book up into project chapters as well as covering the basic techniques and the kind of materials and equipment that you'll find most useful. The projects themselves are divided into six chapters, inspired by some of the reasons and occasions when a bag is needed. Shopping, work or college, luggage, picnicking, days out and crafting are all included but I'm sure that you will see many opportunities for 'cross-pollination' between the chapters and ways you could use my designs for other occasions.

I'm a fabric lover and love to design projects that really celebrate the fabric. I've used lots of different styles of fabric for this book but I suppose each one reflects a side of my character. Even my 'city' bags, although practical and smart, understated and simple, had to have a little bit of zebra and palm tree thrown at them! That's the point isn't it? This is me... now show me who you are!

My bag designs are a great way to show your personality and style but don't stop at the fabric! Every pattern comes with a 'Make it yours...' tip where I share one or two ideas for variations. Add pockets, leave pockets out, mix designs and create hybrids, enlarge or reduce the sizes. Experiment! I want you to use these 21 designs as a starting point in your bag-making journey so feel free – no, I insist – make each one as unique as you are!

MATERIALS, EQUIPMENT AND BASIC TECHNIQUES

If you're already a keen sewer you'll find most of what you need for bag making in your stash. There are, however, a few 'speciality' items of equipment which are worth investing in. If in doubt, check the project you want to make carefully and cross reference the equipment used here. I've divided this first part into four sections: soft stuff, stuff to add structure, metalware or 'hard stuff' and equipment. Even if you're a regular sewer or bag maker it's still worth having a read... you might make a new discovery!

In basic techniques you'll find the techniques you'll use time and time again when you're bag making (or indeed sewing anything). The methods you'll find here are ones I use regularly and they work beautifully for me – I hope they'll do the same for you. Sewing is a melting pot, though, and if you have your own preferred techniques you'd like to substitute for some of mine then do, just read each project thoroughly before you start and make sure any substituted techniques are going to work.

SOFT STUFF

This is usually the stuff that gets us really excited to make a project... we fall in love with a fabric range, feature print or colour scheme. The fabric we choose really affects the look of our finished bag and it's worth remembering that all you have to do is change the fabric to get a completely different look!

FABRICS FOR THE OUTER BAG (A)

The outer part of our bag is the one we are going to spend most time living with so it's worth choosing something you really love. I'm a big fan of quilt-weight cotton fabrics for bag making. They are very easy to work with, come in thousands of colours, designs and themes and are readily available. You can mix solid or plain cottons, large-, medium- and small-scale designs, stripes and 'blenders' or semi-solids. I often mix two or three fabrics in a bag and like to include a large-scale print, a smaller coordinate or stripe and a semi-solid or blender print.

You can also see what's available in the dressmaking or soft furnishing sections of your fabric store – heavy-weight cotton, drill, furnishing fabrics and canvas can all be used for bag making too.

FABRICS FOR THE LINING (B)

Never underestimate the power of a good lining fabric! You'll see the lining every time you delve into your bag for something and the underside of bag flaps are often on show, so pick a fabric that will complement what's on the outside. Cotton and cotton blends are perfect for lining a bag but also keep a lookout for waterproof fabric which is, of course, ideal for toiletry and beach bags and a great choice for shopping bags and totes too.

SPECIALITY FABRICS (C)

Sometimes we need fabrics with special properties for our bags and if your fabric store doesn't carry them, a search online should quickly yield results.

Making bags that are weather resistant, in particular waterproof or splash proof, is a common goal. Oil cloth is a popular choice for bag making as it has a wipe clean surface and comes in lots of fun and attractive prints. Use a Teflon or non-stick foot if you're sewing with oil cloth. Waxed or oiled cotton is less shiny and has more of a retro look but has similar water-resistant properties and is great for day bags and beach bags. Waterproof cotton fabric is brilliant for making splash-proof bags or bags that can withstand a showery day, but the choice of designs and colours can be limited.

Sometimes we need a fabric that we can see through and for that I'll go for either cheesecloth, cotton voile or muslin – particularly if I want the bag to be very light and washable (as in my produce bags). Or I'll use clear vinyl which is, as the name suggests, completely see through, as well as wipeable, making it a brilliant choice for washbags, craft bags and project pouches.

Waffle towelling or towelling is lovely to line a beach or baby bag with as it's naturally moisture wicking and helps to keep the contents dry. Look for towelling with very minimal stretch in it – waffle towelling is extremely stable, easy to sew and looks smart. It's made from cotton too so it can be dyed to any colour you need!

THREAD (E)

Use good-quality thread for your bag-making projects as it's quite literally the stuff that is holding your bag together. Thread is available in cotton, polyester and poly-cotton mixtures. My preference is for blended 'sew-all' or 'dual-duty' threads. There are hundreds of colours to choose from but you can use a small range of neutral beige/tan and grey tones for most construction work. When it comes to top stitching you can use toning or blending colours, add an accent or pop of co-ordinating or contrasting thread or even look for multicoloured or variegated threads. For sewing on buttons or magnetic fastenings I like to use linen thread for its incredible strength and durability.

ZIPS/ZIPPERS (G & F)

A fantastic addition to a bag, zips look smart and give a professional 'polished' look to your makes but also provide security for your belongings and can add a flash of colour just where you need it. Don't be afraid of zips, they are not hard to sew into a bag and you can practise with scrap fabric and a spare zip until you are ready for the real thing! I always use nylon zips as they can be sewn over (with care) and cut to length easily with scissors. Look for regular rather than 'invisible' zips in the haberdashery department. You will sometimes need an open-ended or 'coat' zip – these are widely available and come in lots of colours. As the name suggests, these zips can be fully opened so they are great for bags that you want to open fully, like my picnic bag. If you need to shorten this kind of zip remember to do it from the top end, not the end that you insert into the zip pull. It's also worth looking out for continuous zip or zip on a roll. This is a length – often metres – of zip that comes with a bag of zip pulls so you can make lots of shorter zips. It's also perfect when you need a really long zip, like for my convertible tote 'n' towel beach bag.

VELCRO (H)

This is really useful for the bag maker. It is perfect for a chic, easy and child-friendly bag closure and can be used to secure pocket flaps too. Look for the 'sew and sew' variety – this is really the only kind you want to use for bags. Black and white Velcro is widely available, but if you look hard you might be able to find brights, neons and pastels!

CORDS (I, J & K)

Bags often have a cord to hang, carry or close them, sometimes all three! Cord can be bought in a variety of thicknesses and is available in cotton and nylon/synthetic versions. Cotton cord has a matte finish and can be bleached and dyed to coordinate with your project, although it is most often used in its base colour, a creamy white. Thicker versions look like rope and can be used to give a casual 'beachy' look to projects. Synthetic or nylon cords tend to be whiter and brighter but generally can't be dyed. They are very strong, even in the finest thickness and are ideal when you need super strength without bulk.

WEBBING (D)

Webbing and ready-made handles are worth looking out for; I tend to buy them whenever I see them as I know they'll come in handy! You can buy webbing in a variety of widths and colours and sometimes striped versions by the yard/metre. Ready-made bag handles are available to buy and usually come in pairs. A pattern might need a little adaptation to use them, but the results look professional and can really elevate a simple bag!

STUFF TO ADD STRUCTURE

It's easy to focus on the gorgeous fabrics on the outside of our bags and in the linings but, the truth is, it's the stuff going on inside that really makes our bags look and feel special. There are a variety of different materials that can be used to give our bags structure and shape, depending on the desired finished look and function of the bag.

FUSIBLE FOAM (B) such as Bosal In-R-Form, is my go-to when I need a very structured bag with a padded feel but one which is still very lightweight. Fusible foam comes in single and double-sided, and there are also non-fusible versions. Cut a single layer at a time.

VOLUME BATTING (J) such as Vlieseline H640, comes in a variety of weights and may be fusible or not. It's a little bit like interfacing, with a thin layer of batting or wadding attached to it. It's great for adding padding and soft structure to a bag without adding weight.

QUILT WADDING (BATTING) (F) can be used for giving a soft padded feel to a bag and you can choose between cotton, polyester or a mixture. It won't add much in the way of structure but if you want to make something softly padded it's ideal.

THERMAL INSULATING BATTING (A) such as Thermolam or Insul-Bright from The Warm Company, is a great choice when you want heat retention or insulation, so it's ideal for lunch bags, picnic bags and water bottle carriers. Any batting or wadding will insulate to a certain extent but Thermolam and thermal insulating batting has a special construction and materials which make it extra-insulating.

DECOVIL (H) is a type of interfacing that is very firm and stiff and feels very much like leather. It is bonded to the wrong side of fabric and makes it rigid – perfect for very structured bags and boxes, especially when you want a strong but thin structure. It can also be used in conjunction with volume fleece or quilt batting to get a padded but very firm finish.

DECOVIL LIGHT (G) has a very similar handle to Decovil but is lighter and not so rigid. It still produces very firm results but with more flexibility.

FUSIBLE INTERFACING (C) is a great choice as it is widely available and comes in different weights – light, medium and heavy – depending on the level of structure required. Medium-weight fusible interfacing is a great standby and can be used for shoulder straps and handles too, while heavyweight interfacing offers even more solid structure **(I)**. There is also a version that is gridded on the reverse **(D)** to help with accurate cutting out.

WAIST SHAPER (E) is a great alternative to interfacing for bag handles and shoulder straps and it's fusible too! Originally designed to stiffen waistbands it's also perfect for bag making. It comes in a standard 3" (7.6cm) width that can be trimmed to narrower widths.

METALWARE

The metalware or hardware that we use for our bag making can really elevate a project from homemade to handmade so keep a lookout for gorgeous gold, silver, brass and bronze accessories to dress up your makes. You can buy plastic, ceramic or wooden accessories for bag making too and I've also been known to 'cannibalize' an old bag to liberate the metalware to use in a new bag.

D-RINGS AND RECTANGULAR RINGS (A & B) are the most useful and common types of bag-making metalware. They are used to attach handles, shoulder straps and sometimes closures. Use D-rings with a swivel clip and rectangular rings for fixed straps. They are available in a variety of sizes but my favourite comes with a 1½" (3.8cm) aperture.

SWIVEL CLIPS (C) are very useful and are essentially what you get at the end of a dog lead. They clip onto D-rings and are great when you want a shoulder strap to be removable. They can also be used to close a flap on a messenger-style bag. The larger 2" (5cm) and 1½" (3.8cm) versions are great for shoulder straps, the smaller 1" (2.5cm) and ½" (13mm) are great for closures (as in my essential toiletry bag pattern) or for key savers (as in my overnight attaché).

STRAP SLIDERS (D) are fab! They look like a buckle and sometimes the centre pin slides up and down, but a fixed centre is fine too. They allow the length of a shoulder strap to be altered, allowing a bag to be worn over the shoulder or cross-body. Quick and easy to fit, I promise you'll want to add one to every bag you make! Make sure you buy the same size aperture as your rectangular or D-rings.

EYELETS (E, WITH PUNCH) can be added to the top of a bag to create a drawstring closure (as in my splash proof beach bag) or can be used in conjunction with a tab or tie to make a bag closure. Buy eyelets as a set alongside the fitting tools.

TWIST LOCKS (not shown) are a smart and speedy way to add a closure to a bag with a flap. They can be added as you make the bag or to a finished bag and look very professional.

SPRING LOADED LOCKS (F) are little plastic balls containing a spring-mounted button and a hole to thread cord or ties through and lock them in place. They work really well with drawstring bags, like my produce bags and ultimate knitting and crochet project bag. I like to use spring locks with Roman blind cord as it's the perfect width to go through and creates a very strong drawstring.

BAG FEET (G) can be added to any bag you intend to put on the floor to save the bottom from getting dusty. You install bag feet just like adding a stud or brad. Bag feet come in the same range of colours as other metalware and it's a good idea to match them.

POPPERS/SNAP FASTENERS (H, WITH INSERTION TOOL) are a very quick and easy way to create a closed pocket or flap. You can buy sets of plastic snap fasteners in all sorts of fun and subtle colours to suit your fabrics and the tools you'll need to apply them usually come with the snaps.

MAGNETIC 'SEW-ON' BUCKLES (not shown) always make a bag look so professional. They are added onto a finished bag and are the perfect final touch.

EQUIPMENT

Good basic sewing kit is essential but there are a couple of extra tools you might like to add.

SEWING MACHINE (not shown) all of the bags in this book are made using a sewing machine and I don't recommend attempting to hand sew them because the layers are generally too thick and firm to hand sew with ease. You'll be doing a straight stitch most of the time; it helps if you can adjust the length of the stitch. A zig zag stitch is useful for neatening seams and you'll need a zip foot for sewing zips. A walking foot can be helpful when sewing many thick layers.

MACHINE NEEDLES (A) need to be changed for every new project. Use good-quality machine needles and keep a range of sizes handy. I like size 90 or 100 for bag making. If you're having issues sewing thick layers and your machine is skipping stitches, increase the size of your needle (the higher the number, the thicker the needle).

SCISSORS (B) ideally two pairs – medium or large – for general cutting out and a small fine tipped pair of 'embroidery' scissors for detail cutting and snipping. Make sure you keep your scissors just for cutting fabric.

THREAD SNIPS (C) for cutting threads. Use these and not your scissors!

ROTARY CUTTER/RULER/MAT (D & K) great for cutting strips, squares, rectangles.

TRACING/TISSUE PAPER (not shown) useful for making paper patterns. If you are using scissors to cut out your bag then paper patterns, even for squares and strips, can make the job a lot easier. Look for dressmaker's tissue paper.

HAMMER (not shown) not usually found in your sewing kit but very useful for applying metal eyelets.

EYELET PUNCH TOOLS (see page 17) usually supplied with eyelets or you can buy eyelet punch tools separately if you will be using them a lot.

POPPER/SNAP FASTENER INSTALLING TOOLS (see page 17) these are supplied with your snap fasteners.

PINS (E) I like Clover flat flower head pins. They are long and strong and do a great job of holding thin flat layers together for sewing.

WONDER CLIPS (F) these are ideal when you want to hold multiple or very thick layers together, such as the final putting together of a bag and lining. Around 20–30 is enough for most bag-making projects.

POINT TURNERS/CHOPSTICKS (G) you can buy strap-turning tools and point turners but a simple wooden chopstick does the job beautifully and I always have one to hand!

IRON/PRESSING SURFACE (H) a good heavy iron and firmly padded pressing surface is essential to create neat flat seams and a crisp finish.

QUILT TACKING (BASTING) SPRAY (I) a temporary adhesive aerosol designed to hold layers of fabric and wadding (batting) together. It can also be used to add non-fusible interfacing to fabric and to temporarily hold appliqués and decorative elements in place. Follow the manufacturer's instructions and only use a type designed for tacking quilt layers.

SEAM RIPPER (J) a small tool with a sharp curved blade for cutting through stitches to unpick a seam.

STILETTO (not shown) a sharply pointed tool for piercing holes for eyelets and snap fasteners. A thick darning needle could be substituted.

FREEZER PAPER (not shown) thick, white matt paper with a shiny waxed reverse side. The waxy side is ironed onto fabric and can be removed without leaving residue. It is useful for templates and making repeated and accurate folds in fabric.

FABRIC MARKERS (not shown) either erasable or non-erasable – test on a spare scrap of fabric first.

BASIC TECHNIQUES

GENERAL TIPS

FABRIC

The bags in this book are all made with 100% cotton fabric. It's super easy to work with, comes in awesome designs and presses and washes really well. I'm all about making life easy so I avoid fabrics with stretch or ones which are terribly thick and would make for a bulky and difficult project. The fabric used is generally 42" (107cm) wide. If you're matching patterns, checks or large repeats you may need more fabric.

Some projects use a long quarter or a fat quarter. A long quarter is a regular ¼ yard (metre) of fabric cut across the width of fabric, yielding a long skinny piece of fabric perfect for making bags with smaller pieces or shoulder straps. A fat quarter is a cut you will likely find in a quilt shop or fabric store. A half yard (metre) of fabric is cut in half again down the centre, yielding two pieces of fabric each approximately 18" x 21" (46 x 53cm) – a quarter of a metre of fabric but "fat" instead of "long". Perfect when you need to cut larger pattern pieces like a bag front or a large pocket.

As far as colours and patterns go, the sky is quite literally the limit. Use patterns and colours that make your heart sing and bring joy to your soul. Making your own bags is a brilliant way to express your personality, so feel free to completely ignore the fabric choices I've made in favour of something that speaks to and about you! One piece of advice though – if you're going to use directional fabrics, stripes and plaids or checks, think carefully about how you will cut them out before you reach for your scissors. I love to use bold and often directional prints but I often restrict them to bag fronts, pockets or flaps – the pieces are large and show off the prints well, I don't have the headache of matching patterns across numerous seams and it makes the print a real focal point. Easy impact without any hassle!

And finally… give your fabrics a good press before you start cutting out. Steam press if you can, it'll tighten the fabric up and mean that any shrinkage is likely to happen before you cut your pattern pieces.

CUTTING OUT ↓

The vast majority of the pattern pieces in this book are rotary cut. They are based on strips and large squares or rectangles. If you're not sure about rotary cutting read on, we cover that in this chapter. If you'd rather go old-school and use scissors, that will work perfectly too… just measure and mark out the shapes on your fabric with tailor's chalk or a marking pen, then cut the pieces out with dressmaking scissors.

If a project calls for a paper pattern, just trace the pattern piece template (see pull-out pattern sheet) onto dressmaker's tissue paper which you've ironed first to remove wrinkles. Rough cut the paper pattern and pin to the fabric. Cut out pattern pieces and fabrics in one go, following the line. All seam allowances are included unless stated otherwise.

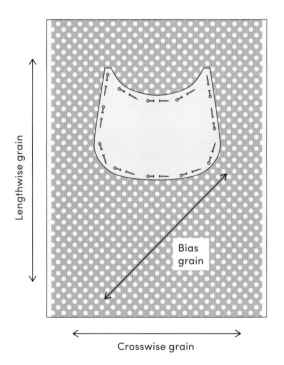

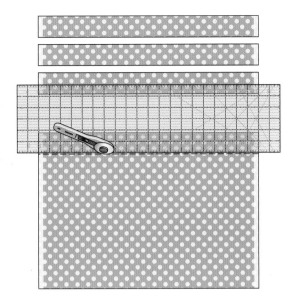

Most of your pattern pieces need to be cut out with straight sides on the 'straight of grain' – parallel to the selvedge on your fabric. If you're using a printed fabric you'd naturally do this anyway so that the patterns on your fabric are the right way up and 'straight'. Cutting pattern pieces on the straight of grain ensures that the edges stay straight and don't stretch out of shape when you're sewing, as the lengthwise and crosswise grainlines are most stable. Where possible cut shoulder straps on the lengthwise grain (running North to South along the selvedge) as this is the most stable grainline and there is little or no stretch. Occasionally we need to cut on the bias (see opposite below).

ROTARY CUTTING

You can use a rotary cutter, perspex gridded ruler and self-healing mat to cut pieces for bags quickly and accurately. You can cut up to four layers of fabric at a time and, with a little practise rotary cutting, can really speed up the bag-making process. Lay the ruler onto your fabric and make sure it is lined up with the straight of grain. Next align the rotary cutter blade with the edge of the ruler and push the rotary cutter forward with a firm downward press to cut through the fabric. Use the ruler to measure out your cuts. Always cut away from yourself and turn the board and the fabric as one unit in order to cut the remaining sides of your bag panel. Alternatively, mark out the shape you want to cut with tailor's chalk or a marking pencil, then cut along the lines with the rotary cutter and ruler.

CUTTING FABRIC ON THE BIAS ←

Sometimes we need to embrace fabric's weird ability to stretch. There's very little stretch in the lengthwise or crosswise grains of woven fabric but cut fabric at a 45° angle and the picture is very different! Cutting through the warp and weft means that the edges of the fabric stretch quite a bit – this is brilliant when we need to sew a binding around a curved edge. Line up the 45° mark on your rotary ruler with a straight edge on your fabric. The cutting edge of your ruler will be positioned across your fabric at a 45° angle. Simply cut along the ruler's edge and then cut your binding strips from that edge. Watch how you handle fabrics cut on the bias – be gentle with them or they will stretch out of shape and then the edges will go frilly, not the look we are going for! To join bias strips, place at right angles as shown and seam. Press the seam open and trim off the little triangles each side.

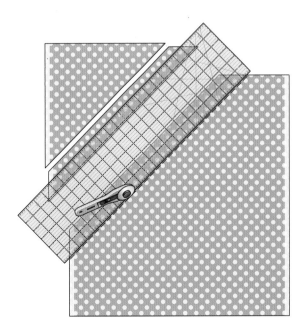

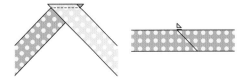

SEWING SEAMS

Seams come in different widths. It often depends on what you're making or who's written the pattern. Accuracy is important to ensure your pieces fit together well so read each project carefully. You might like to underline the seam allowances used at various stages. For the most part I've used a ¼" (6mm) seam allowance, occasionally its ⅜" (10mm) or ½" (13mm), but I'll always let you know.

I like to use a shorter than average stitch length when I'm making bags. The seams take a lot of strain and a shorter stitch length will make for a stronger bag. Set the stitch length to 1.8–2.0 for construction seams. When it comes to decorative top stitching I prefer to use a longer stitch length, 3.0 is perfect I think, just remember to go back down to 1.8–2.0 when you return to construction.

ADDING INTERFACING →

A lot of the bags in this book have a layer of interfacing added to make the fabric firmer. I like to use fusible interfacing which you iron onto the wrong side of your chosen fabric. The standard width for interfacing is usually around 30" (76.2cm). It is always better to over-buy, so that you never run out! Whichever interfacing you use will come with instructions for fusing, usually printed on the edge of the interfacing. Use the correct heat – I like medium/ two spot and steam or I'll cover the interfacing with a damp cloth. Take your time when you're ironing interfacing, the 'bond' isn't instant. It'll take up to 15 seconds of continuous heat, but don't take my word for it – always follow the manufacturer's instructions! I like to cut interfacing ¼" (6mm) smaller on all sides than the piece of fabric I'm sticking it to. That means that the fabric in the seam allowances isn't bulked out with the extra couple of layers. It takes a little longer to cut out, and you'll have to cut fabrics and interfacing separately, but I think that it's worth the extra step.

Experiment with interfacing – even quilt-weight cottons vary in thickness and firmness. Try different weights of interfacing until you get the level of firmness that suits your project.

Waist shaper is added in the same way. Cut it ½" (13mm) narrower than the shoulder strap and fuse it with ¼" (6mm) of fabric showing either side. When I'm applying fusible foam (such as In-R-Form), I cut this to the same size as the fabric it is to be bonded to. It's important that the foam is caught in the seams. If you find your seams are getting bulky you can trim a little of the foam away from the seam allowances after you have sewn them. Use sharp scissors to do this. In general, I don't find this necessary but it's always an option and will not affect the durability of your project.

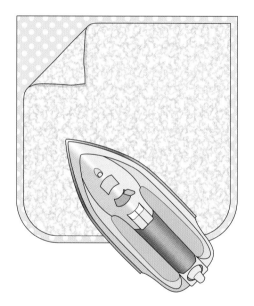

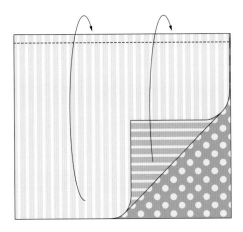

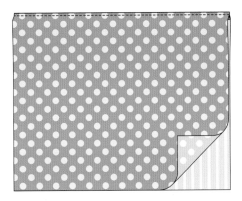

Patch (slip) pocket

SEWING A BASIC PATCH (SLIP) POCKET AND ONE WITH FAUX BINDING

A patch pocket is one which is completely flat and can either be inserted into a seam, usually in the lining, or can 'float' on another piece. A patch pocket is made by sewing two pieces of fabric together of equal size, one for the outer and one for the lining. Once the top seam has been sewn and the seam allowances pressed open, the fabrics are opened out and the lining and outer fabrics placed wrong sides together with the top seam creating a 'knife edge'. The top edge is usually top stitched at this point about ⅛" (3mm) in from this upper seam and then the pocket is tacked (basted) to the bag. The raw edges at the bottom and sides will be caught into the side and base seams. If the pocket is to 'float' outside of the seam lines, the side and bottom seam allowances will need to be turned in by ¼" (6mm) and pressed. Then the sides and bottom edges can be sewn onto the corresponding back section. First sew very close to the folded edge and then again ¼" (6mm) in from this line of stitching, thus enclosing the raw edges inside the pocket – a neat and very easy finish! You can add patch pockets to many of the bags in this book if you need them!

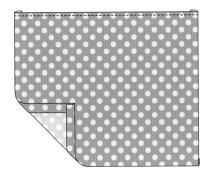

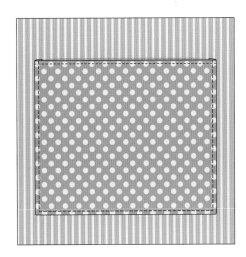

Floating pocket

I also like to make patch (slip) pockets with a faux binding. The outer pocket piece is cut to one size but the lining is a little longer – generally with ½" (13mm) extra; the top edges are stitched together and the seam allowance is pressed up towards the lining, then the lining is flipped back, over the seam allowance and back down the other side. The bottom edges should meet perfectly and you will be left with around ¼" (6mm) of the lining showing on the right side, creating a gorgeous faux binding effect. A line of top stitching just into this binding completes the illusion that a separate binding has been applied and it's a lovely opportunity to add a little colour accent to an otherwise quite plain bag. Patch pockets with faux binding can be substituted for any regular patch pocket so have fun and make each bag uniquely yours!

→

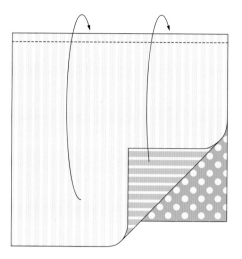

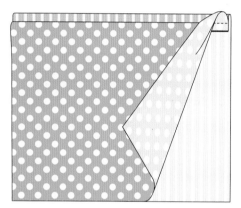

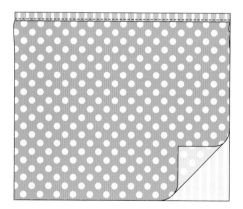

Patch (slip) pocket with faux binding

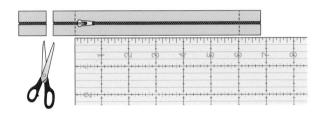

ZIPS

Zips and bags are a natural fit! Zips keep things secure and who wouldn't want to keep the contents of their bag safe? Zips cause many sewers a flutter of nerves but there's absolutely no need to feel anxious – zips are easy to master! Buy a 10" (25cm) or 12" (30cm) zip, grab some scrap fabrics and practise a few times at least before you tackle the same job in one of the bags.

SHORTENING ZIPS ←

Sometimes you have the perfect zip – the right colour and style – but it's too long. Not a problem! Measure the length you need from the top of the zip pull down towards the stop, and mark a line with pencil. Use your sewing machine and a straight stitch to sew across your marked line three or four times to create a new stop. Trim the excess zip away leaving about ½" (13mm) allowance. It's a great idea to do this line of stitching at the top end too – just pull the zipper pull down out of the way, bring the ends of the zip back together and stitch back and forth a few times. This will ensure that when you insert the zip and need to open it, the ends won't splay open!

MAKING ZIP ENDS ←

Zip ends add a really professional touch to a zip and help it to blend in or stand out from the rest of the bag. Zip ends can also be used to make your zip just a little longer, meaning your 9" (22.9cm) zip will fit a 10" (25.4cm) bag top!

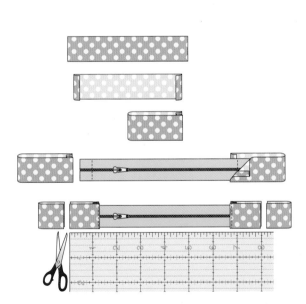

Cut two strips of fabric the width of your zip (most often 1"/2.5cm) and 5" (12.7cm) in length), and press a ¼" (6mm) in at both short ends to neaten. Fold the strip in half, wrong sides together and press. Slip one end of your zip into the neatened ends so that your ¼" (6mm) seam allowance covers about ½" (13mm) of the zip tape. Carefully top stitch across the neatened ends through all layers. Snip through the fold and trim away the extra zip from the seam allowance. Repeat the process at the other end of the zip. Trim the neatened zip to the required length, keeping the amount of zip 'end' equal at both ends.

SEWING A SIMPLE ZIP →

These are your 'bread and butter' zips. Perfect for adding a zip to the top of a pouch bag or to the back or front of a plain bag.

Cut two pieces of fabric for the top of the zip – one outer and one lining piece, the same size as each other – and cut the same for the bottom of the zip. Most of the time this 'top and bottom' will actually be the front and back of the bag, depending on the specific project.

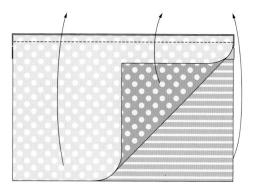

Sandwich one side of the zip between the outer and lining fabrics for the top with right sides of the fabrics together. Use a zipper foot on your sewing machine to sew along the raw edges. Sew a scant ¼" (6mm).

Open the lining and outer fabrics up and press them back away from the zip, then fold them back on themselves so that wrong sides are touching. Match the side and bottom edges of your outer and lining carefully and press, then top stitch very close to the zip, again using your zipper foot.

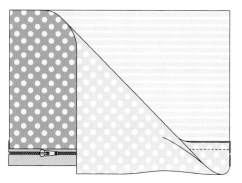

Repeat this process on the other side of the zip.

If you're nervous about sewing the outer and lining in one step, you can always sew the outer to the zip first then add the lining. Sew a tiny bit further in than your first line of stitching to make sure you don't see those stitches!

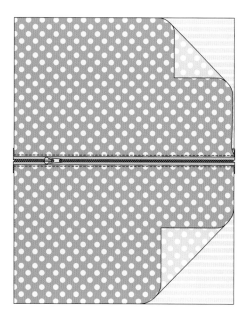

ADDING FABRIC SIDES TO A ZIP ←

Sometimes I'll add fabric sides to a zip before sewing it to the rest of the pocket or the bag. Most often I'll do this with vinyl pockets, which by their very nature are unlined. Adding sides to a zip completely encloses them and neatens them beautifully – and it makes a real feature of your zip!

Start with a rectangle of fabric. I always cut mine a bit longer than my zip and then trim later. The width will be specified in the project. Press a ¼" (6mm) in on one of the long edges of the fabric. Sew the other long edge to one side of the zip, right side of the fabric against the right side of the zip, raw edges aligned, just as if you were sewing a basic zip (see opposite). Press the fabric back away from the zip but don't top stitch yet! Turn the neatened edge of the fabric to the back of the zip and just cover the first row of stitching with the neatened edge of your fabric. From the front of your work, top stitch very close to the edge of the zip, attaching the fabric at the back at the same time. Press the top edge of the fabric neatly. Most often you will repeat this process on the other side of the zip. Trim the ends of the fabric sides even with the zip or to the required length in the project.

MAKING A LETTERBOX ZIP →

A letterbox zip is a sleek and professional looking closure to a pocket and has the advantage of being part of the 'body' of the bag. It can be used on the inside or the outside of a bag.

Cut two rectangles of fabric for the lining of the pocket, both the same size. On the wrong side of one of the rectangles draw a rectangular 'letterbox', which will usually be the length of your zip by ½" (13mm) wide.

Position this marked fabric piece right side down onto the right side of your bag panel in the specified position. Sew around the 'letterbox', making sure that you sew right on your drawn lines and pivoting at each of the four corners. I like to use a shorter stitch than normal: 1.8–2.0 in length. Carefully cut down the centre of your 'letterbox' and also snip into the corners. Cut to the line of stitching but not through it! Turn the rectangle of fabric through the letterbox and press the edges really crisply and neatly. I like to do this with my fingers first, get a great finish and then go to my iron and press everything really flat.

Tack (baste) the zip in place behind the 'letterbox' so that the right side of the zip is showing on the right side of the back. I like to hand tack the zip in place, then sew around the zip from the right side using the sewing machine and a zipper foot. Working from the wrong side, pin the other rectangle of lining fabric to the first with right sides together, being sure to keep the pocket linings away from the body of the bag. Sew around the edges of the pinned rectangles to join them together. Continue making the bag.

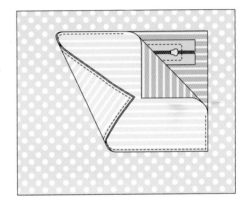

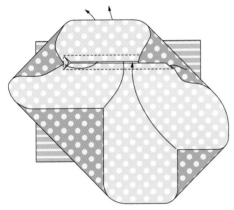

BINDING

Bindings are used to add a decorative edging to pockets and the tops of some bags, and they can also be used to finish the edges of a quilted project. There are two different binding methods you might find useful. I always neaten one short end of my binding by folding in ½" (13mm) and pressing, then I'll simply slip the other raw end of the binding under this fold to neaten the ends.

SINGLE FOLD BINDING →

Start by cutting strips of fabric that are 1¼" (3.2cm) wide by the length you need. I always cut extra length to make the binding strip easier to handle. Fold and press the strip in half, wrong sides together, unfold the binding and then turn a ¼" (6mm) hem on the other long raw edge and press. Lay the binding on the edge to be bound, working from the outside of your bag or pocket, right sides together and raw edges aligned. Sew a ¼" (6mm) seam allowance to attach the binding to the bag. Fold the binding up and over the raw edge to cover it, bringing the other neatened edge down over the back of your work. It should sit slightly lower than your first line of stitching, thereby covering it. Pin the binding in place then sew the binding to the back of your work by hand. Alternatively top stitch from the front, sewing very close to the bottom edge of the binding to catch the binding at the back. Single fold binding is great to use on areas of medium to light use and also uses half as much fabric as double fold binding, so if fabric is in short supply use this method.

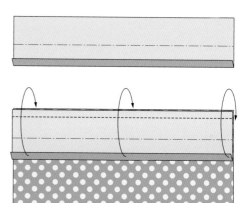

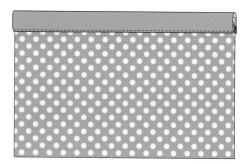

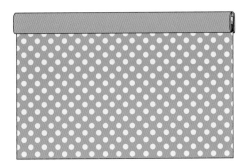

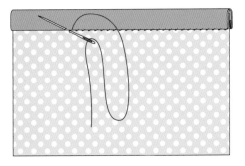

DOUBLE FOLD BINDING ←

Start with a binding strip that is 2½" (6.2cm) wide by the required length. Again, I always cut extra length. Fold the strip in half lengthwise, wrong sides together. Align the two raw edges of your binding to the raw edge of your bag, pocket or quilt and sew a ¼" (6mm) seam allowance. Turn the folded fabric up and over the raw edge and slip stitch the binding to the back of your work. Double fold binding is a thicker, more robust binding and is perfect for edges that will suffer very heavy wear and tear.

STRAPS AND TABS

Most of the bags in this book have a strap of some kind and often there are tabs holding metalware (such as D-rings and swivel clips) in place. I use two methods for making mine.

MAKING NARROW STRAPS AND TABS →

For a narrow strap or tab, cut a strip of fabric and then press it in half longways, wrong sides together. Open out the fold and then turn the low raw edges in to meet the centre crease. Press again. Finally fold the strip in half down the original centre fold to enclose the outer raw edges. Top stitch carefully down both of the long sides.

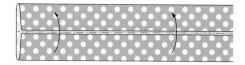

If you need the short ends neatened too, turn and press a ½" (13mm) hem on the strip as step one and then follow the instructions above.

MAKING WIDER TABS AND STRAPS →

For wider straps, cut two strips of fabric. You might well like to interface the outer fabric with interfacing or waist shaper (see page 22) for a stiffer, firmer finish. Place the two strips of fabric right sides together and sew both long edges and one short edge, leaving one narrow end unsewn.

At the short sewn end make a deep indentation with your thumb and then push a chopstick into this hollow. Rest the end of the chopstick on a table and pull the strap down onto the chopstick until the short sewn end is pushed right through the open end. Grab the neatened end and pull the whole strap through to the right side. Press your strap carefully and then top stitch the long edges very close to the seams. Cut this strap down to make shorter lengths, if required.

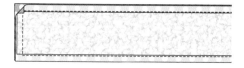

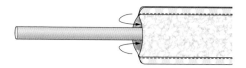

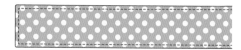

MAKING STRAP POCKETS ←

I often make little 'pockets' to tuck straps and D-ring attachments into.

I do this when I'm not inserting the end of the strap into a seam. Pockets are an easy and smart looking way to cover the raw ends of a strap and they are quick to make! Take a small rectangle of fabric and fold in a ¼" (6mm) hem on each short end. Press. Fold the rectangle in half with right sides together so that the two neatened ends are together and sew down the sides. Back stitch at the ends. Turn through to the right side and press. That's it! Now tuck the end of the strap into the pocket and sew the whole thing to your bag, as instructed.

SEWING A CROSS FOR STRENGTH

Use this technique when you are attaching straps to bags, sewing on strap pockets or when finishing the ends of an adjustable strap slider for a very strong and durable join.

You're going to sew a box with a cross through the middle – you can mark this with an erasable marker if you wish or, just eyeball it! Start by bringing your bobbin thread to the top and hold both top and bobbin threads as you start stitching – this is to prevent a 'bird's nest' forming on the back of your work. Stitch forward and back a couple of times to secure your thread, then sew the outside box shape. Once you get back to the start, sew diagonally through the middle to the opposite corner, sew the bottom of the box for a second time, then sew diagonally again to the opposite corner. Finally sew back across the top and reverse a couple of stitches to secure.

ADDING AN ADJUSTABLE STRAP SLIDER →

These are the perfect addition to any shoulder strap where you need the length to be adjustable. A cross body messenger bag is a great example. Most of the time I wear mine across my body, but occasionally I need the strap to be shorter so I can wear it on my shoulder. Strap sliders look like a buckle and are fitted in quite a similar way.

Attach one end of the shoulder strap to the bag as normal: thread it through the rectangular ring, overlap the end of the strap and sew with a 'cross'. Now thread your strap slider onto the strap and slide it about halfway along the strap. Poke the unattached end of the strap through the other rectangular ring and then form the shoulder strap into a circle, doubling the strap back on itself. Pass the unattached end through the back of the strap slider, passing it over the centre bar. Bring the end of the strap back onto the strap, matching lining side to lining side. This should be about 4" (10cm) away from the strap slider. Pin in place, then sew a cross to attach the strap.

1

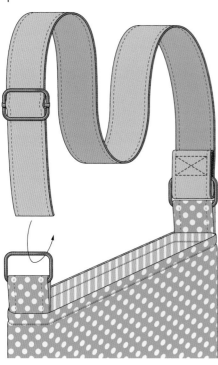

2

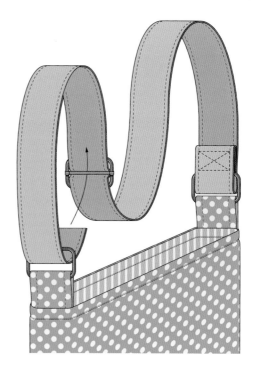

3

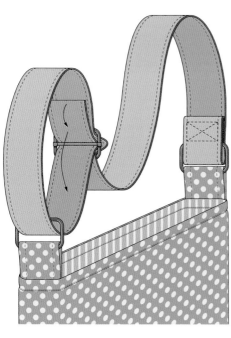

4

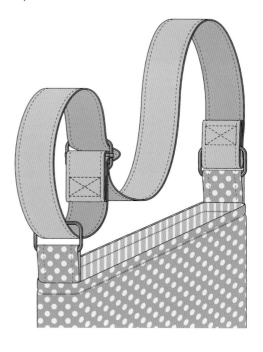

SHAPE AND STRUCTURE

Bags need structure so that they can hold all your things. These are my favourite techniques for quickly bringing shape to flat pieces of fabric.

BOXING CORNERS →

This is a brilliant technique for adding depth and shape to a bag which is essentially two flat rectangles sewn together. Sew the side and base seams first, just as if you were making a flat tote. Use a ruler to mark a square at each of the bottom corners. The size will be given in the project but generally this will be 1"–3" (2.5–7.6cm). Cut the squares away using sharp scissors. Bring the side and base seam together on one of the corners, bringing the cut edges together into a straight line. Sew this seam. Repeat on the other corner and you're done! Occasionally a pattern might instruct you to cut the corners away first and then sew the side and base seams – if you're doing this just remember to leave the sides of the square un-sewn!

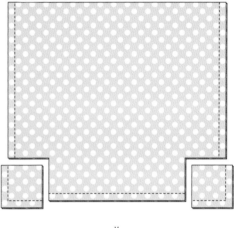

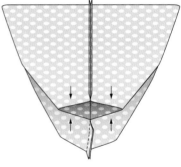

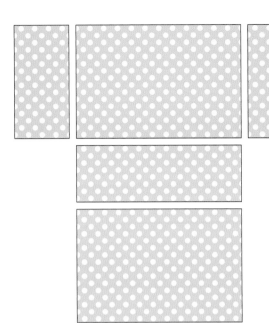

MAKING A BOX BAG ←

A box bag has a front and a back and then three separate pieces to create a gusset. I prefer to use the separate pieces as it makes it really easy to achieve perfect corners. This is my favourite shape to use for bags – it doesn't require pattern pieces, it can be simply rotary cut and the smart corners are really easy to achieve, just follow my tips and techniques.

Set your pieces out into a T-shape then sew the front panel to the base panel with right sides together. Start and finish your ¼" (6mm) seam allowance ¼" (6mm) in from each end and backstitch to secure. Sew the back to the base panel in the same way.

Sew the side panels to the back bag. Start sewing right at the very top of the bag and sew down to ¼" (6mm) from the bottom. Backstitch as before. Repeat this on all four side seams to create a box.

Finally sew the bottom side seams, starting and finishing your seams ¼" (6mm) in from the ends and backstitching to secure.

TIP: You don't have to guess where ¼" (6mm) from the end is! Measure and mark a pencil dot to show you where to start and finish.

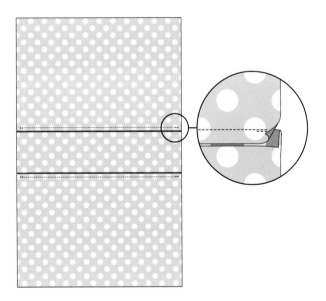

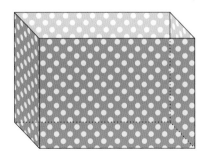

LINING YOUR BAGS

Most of the time I make a separate bag lining, made in exactly the same way as the outer bag but with a gap in one of the seams. I leave a gap that is about four fingers wide – if I can get four fingers through the gap it will be big enough to turn anything through. The outer bag is then placed inside the lining, right sides together, and the top seam is sewn, joining the outer and lining together. The bag is turned through the gap and once I've checked the top seam to make sure everything is looking good, I can close the gap in the lining, either by hand with small invisible slip stitches or by machine, simply bringing the neatened edges of the gap together and sewing very close to the edge.

Sometimes the lining can be dropped inside a bag, wrong side to wrong side, and then the edges need to be bound. This is also how a quilt or quilted bag is finished. Refer to the binding techniques on pages 30–31 for how to do this.

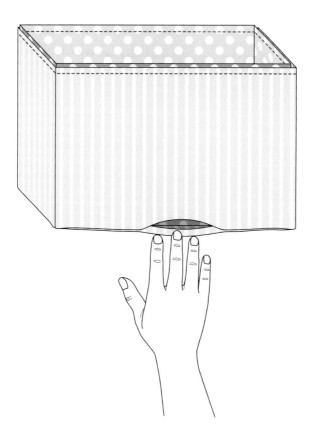

FINISHING TOUCHES

Hardware really gives your bag a professional look – choose from the many finishes available and follow my advice to add that final touch.

ADDING FEET TO A BAG

Bag feet are added to the base of a bag that might well spend a lot of its time on the floor. The picnic bag has them, and they could be added to the weekend warrior bag. Bag feet look very much like large studs, the kind you might find on a biker's leather jacket! Each foot has a couple of metal prongs. Layer your outer fabric with batting or foam and then mark a dot where the feet will be positioned. Make a small hole through the dot and push the prongs of the bag foot from right side to wrong side. Open out the prongs on the wrong side of the base to secure the foot. If you're not using batting or foam, make sure the bag is interfaced with a medium to firm interfacing and add an extra 2" (5cm) squares of interfacing where you will be adding feet. Make the hole through all these layers and then add the feet.

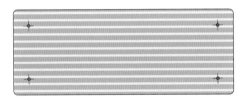

ADDING POPPERS/ SNAP FASTENERS

Plastic snap fasteners are a recent discovery for me and have been something of a revelation! They are a brilliantly quick and super easy way to close a bag or pocket or add something which is removable. The tools and snap fasteners come together in a kit. The fastener has a male and female part and both require a cover which looks like a drawing pin (thumb tack). Make a tiny hole using a bradawl and pass the pin part through the hole. Add the male or female part to the pin and then cover both with the setting pliers and squeeze to crush the pin and male or female part together.

ADDING EYELETS

Metal eyelets come in a variety of finishes and are a great way to add a 'hole' to a bag – perfect for threading a drawstring through, as in my splash proof sling bag. Mark the position of your eyelets and then use the hole cutting tool (included with your eyelets) and a hammer to bash a hole through the fabrics. You might need a pair of embroidery scissors to cut the hole out perfectly. Place the two halves of an eyelet through the hole and then place onto the setting tool. Another quick bash with a hammer will crush the two halves of the eyelet together and encase the raw edges of the hole.

A TRIP TO THE MARKET

Shopping bags have undergone something of a makeover in recent years. We've all embraced the need to banish as much single-use plastic as we can, and one of the easiest and most effective ways to do this is to use our own shopping bags!

Nothing beats a trip to the farmers' market. Buying locally produced food and chatting to the growers is one of my favourite ways to spend a Saturday morning and my produce bags are the perfect thing to take for fruits and veggies – of course, they work perfectly at the supermarket too and make great quick gifts for friends.

My expanding shopping totes replace the need for a plastic bag and hold just as much as any 'bag for life' but mine can be made in your favourite prints and colours and roll into a tiny bundle just right for keeping in your pocket or handbag.

Small but perfectly formed, my tri-fold wallet is the ultimate organizer for cash, cards and travel passes and is a stylish and rewarding make.

Finally, for really big shopping trips, my trolley bags will make packing and keeping your produce beautifully organized a dream!

SHOPPING TROLLEY BAGS

Even a trip to the supermarket can be stylish and practical with my shopping trolley bags. One set of four bags does it all. Whether you use a small trolley or a full-sized one, the bags expand to fit and can be packed and organized at the checkout. My bags, which come in two sizes, are super sturdy and will cope admirably with heavy items.

In this project we will make sturdy handles with reinforcing strap pockets and sew a box bag.

FINISHED SIZES

	Base	Height	Extended height
Small	13½" x 6½" (34.3 x 16.5cm)	8" (20.3cm)	16" (40.6cm)
Large	17½" x 6½" (44.5 x 16.5cm)	10" (25.4cm)	20" (50.8cm)

CUTTING

Both sizes of bag are made in exactly the same way but there is a 1" (2.5cm) difference in the placement of the handles. Cutting instructions are for one bag.

SMALL BAG
From the lower section fabric cut:
- Front and back panels: two 8½" x 14" (21.6 x 35.5cm) rectangles, landscape
- Side panels: two 8½" x 7" (21.6 x 17.8cm) rectangles, portrait
- Base: one 7" x 14" (17.8 x 35.5cm) rectangle, landscape

Cut exactly the same pieces in fusible foam. Iron to the wrong side of all the corresponding lower section pieces (see Techniques, page 22).

→

Gather your supplies! You will need...

- Fabric

  Lower bag sections and handle: 19¾" (0.5m) for each small bag / 29½" (¾m) for each large bag

  Upper bag sections and handles: 19¾" (0.5m) for each small bag / 29½" (¾m) for each large bag

  Lining: 19¾" (0.5m) for each small bag /29½" (¾m) for each large bag

- Fusible foam (such as Bosal In-R-Form): 58" x 19¾" (1.5 x 0.5m) for either size

- Medium-weight fusible interfacing: 19¾" (0.5m) for either size

- Waist shaper: 3" x 49" (8cm x 1¼m), split down the middle

- Thread to match your fabrics

I used a navy blue dot cotton fabric for the lower bag sections and handles, and four different Ikat-style cotton fabrics for the upper bag sections and handles. For the lining, I used a cream and blue dot cotton print, but solids work well for linings too.

From the upper section fabric cut:
- Front and back panels: two 8½" x 14" (21.6 x 35.5cm) rectangles, landscape
- Side panels: two 8½" x 7" (21.6 x 17.8cm) rectangles, portrait

Cut exactly the same pieces in interfacing. Iron to the wrong side of all the corresponding upper section pieces (see Techniques, page 22).

From both the lower and upper fabrics cut:
- Handles: two 2" x 42" (5 x 106.7cm) strips (four in total)

Interface one strip of each fabric (total of two): iron a 1½" (3.8cm) strip of waist shaper down the centre of the two strips (see Techniques, page 22).
- Four 3" (7.6cm) squares (eight in total)

From the lining fabric cut:
- Two 14" x 16½" (35.5 x 42cm) rectangles
- Two 7" x 16½" (17.8x 42cm) rectangles
- One 7" x 14" (17.8 x 35.5cm) rectangle

LARGE BAG
From the lower section fabric cut:
- Front and back panels: two 10½" x 18" (26.7 x 45.7cm) rectangles, landscape
- Side panels: two 10½" x 7" (26.7 x 17.8cm) rectangles, portrait
- Base: one 7" x 18" (17.8 x 45.7cm) rectangle, landscape

Cut exactly the same pieces in fusible foam. Iron to the wrong side of all the corresponding lower section pieces (see Techniques, page 22).

From the upper section fabric cut:
- Front and back panels: two 10½" x 18" (26.7 x 45.7cm) rectangles, landscape
- Side panels: two 10½" x 7" (26.7 x 17.8cm) rectangles, portrait

Cut exactly the same pieces in interfacing. Iron to the wrong side of all the corresponding upper section fabric pieces (see Techniques, page 22).

From both the lower and upper fabrics cut:
- Handles: two 2" x 42" (5 x 106.7cm) strips (four in total)

Interface one strip each of fabric (total of two): iron a 1½" (3.8cm) strip of waist shaper down the centre of the two strips (see Techniques, page 22).
- Four 3" (7.6cm) squares (eight in total)

From the lining fabric cut:
- Two 18" x 20½" (45.7 x 52cm) rectangles
- Two 7" x 20½" (17.8 x 52cm) rectangles
- One 7" x 18" (17.8 x 45.7cm) rectangle

```
Make it yours...

Both the small and large
trolley bags make great single
bags to take for shopping,
work or leisure activities.
With the benefit of doubling
in size, there are so many
applications for this design!
```

LET'S MAKE THE BAG!

1 Take two of the handle strips cut from the lower section fabric, one should be interfaced with waist shaper and one not. Lay them right sides together and sew along both long edges and one short edge, using a ¼" (6mm) seam allowance.

2 Turn through to the right side and press. Top stitch ⅛" (3mm) along each of the long sides and then cut the strip into two 21" (53.3cm) handles. Repeat this process using the two strips of upper section fabric and set aside.

3 Make the strap pockets. These are great little pockets to slip handles in when there isn't a seam to insert them into. Take one of the 3" (7.6cm) squares of fabric and fold in a ¼" (6mm) seam allowance on each short end. Fold it in half, right sides together. Press. Sew along the short sides, using a ¼" (6mm) seam allowance, and reinforce your stitching at the top/non-folded end. Turn through to the right side, push out the corners and press. Repeat with the remaining seven squares to make a total of eight strap pockets. (See Techniques, page 33.)

4 Slip the raw ends of each bag handle into the strap pockets. I mixed the fabrics up on my bags for contrast. Pin the handles and strap pockets onto the right side of the front and back panels of the upper and lower bag: ½" (13mm) down from the top edge and 2¼" (5.7cm) in from the side edges for the small bag and 3¼" (8.3cm) in from the side edges for the large bag.

5 Sew the strap pockets/handles to the bag panels. Sew ⅛" (3mm) in, all around the pockets, enclosing the folded over top edge as you go, creating a little 'box'. Then sew an X through the centre of the box to reinforce and strengthen the handle. Repeat with all handles.

6 Sew one of the upper bag fronts to the top of one of the lower bag fronts, right sides together, using a ¼" (6mm) seam. Make sure the handles are pinned down out of the way. Flip the top section back, press and top stitch ⅛" (3mm) above the seam. Repeat with the back panels and both of the side panels.

7 Referring to Making a Box Bag instructions on page 37, use a ⅜" (10mm) seam allowance for the final construction of the bag. Sew the front panel of the bag to the base. Start and finish your seam ⅜" (10mm) in from the edge.

8 Sew the back panel to the base in the same way. Sew a side panel to the front panel. Match the mid-point seam carefully. Start sewing at the very top of the bag but finish the seam ⅜" (10mm) before the base. Repeat this step, sewing the other edge of the side panel to the back panel.

9 Finally sew the side panel to the base panel. Start and finish at the ⅜" (10mm) mark. Repeat with the other side panel. Turn your bag to the right side. Press.

10 Make the lining. Use a ⅜" (10mm) seam allowance. Sew the large front and back panels to the base. Start and finish ⅜" (10mm) in, as before. Leave a 6" (15.2cm) gap for turning in the centre of one of these seams. Repeat to add the side panels, and join the side and base panels together. Leave the lining wrong side out.

11 Insert the outer bag into the lining, right sides together, and pin around the top of the bag. Sew around the top of the bag with a ¼" (6mm) seam allowance, being careful not to catch the handles in the seam. Turn to the right side and press. Slip stitch the gap in the lining.

12 Top stitch around the top of the bag to secure the lining and neaten.

To use as half bags, push the upper bag and lining down into the lower bag and smooth out. To use as full bags, simply pull up the handles of the upper bag to bring the sides up!

TRI-FOLD WALLET

House your credit, debit and store cards, loose change, notes, travel passes and even a notebook and pencil in my super handy tri-fold wallet. Getting organized has never looked so stylish and it's easier than you might think!

In this project we will use two different kinds of interfacing, heavy- and medium-weight, make a letterbox zip pocket, make a pocket flap and apply poppers/snap fasteners.

FINISHED SIZES

Folded: 6" x 4½" (15 x 11.5cm), approx
Unfolded: 6" x 13½" (15 x 34cm), approx

CUTTING

In this project we will cut and piece different sections of the wallet one at a time to keep things organized.

LET'S MAKE THE WALLET!

1 ← Start by making the credit card pockets. Cut a strip of freezer paper 4¼" x 22½" (10.8 x 57.2cm) then measure and mark off sections at 2" (5cm), 1¾" (4.4cm), 2" (5cm), 1¾" (4.4cm), and so on, until you have 10 sections, and then finish with a 2" (5cm) section – there should be 11 in total. There will be a little paper left over, that's a little insurance policy for later! Fold the strip of paper and crease the marked lines as shown. Unfold the paper.

Gather your supplies! You will need…

• Fabric

  Inner pockets and outside of wallet: three long quarters in assorted prints

  Lining, accent strips and pocket lining/faux binding: one long quarter in a contrast print

• Medium-weight fusible interfacing: 9¾" (0.25m)

• Heavy-weight fusible interfacing: 6½" x 14" (16.5 x 35.5cm)

• One 8" (20.3cm) zip

• Two plastic poppers/snap fasteners and tools

• Thread to match your fabrics

• Freezer paper

• Stiletto

I used two different Ikat-style fabrics for the inner pockets, a different Ikat print for the outside of the wallet, and a navy script print for the lining, accent strips and pocket lining.

2   Cut a strip of fabric from one of the long quarters for the credit card pockets, 4¼" (10.8cm) wide and about 24" (61cm) in length. Iron the freezer paper to the wrong side of the fabric, centred. Trim the excess fabric, allowing an extra ¼" (6mm) of fabric at either end of the paper.

3   ↓ Fold the strip of fabric up, using the folds in the paper as your guide, and press. Carefully remove the freezer paper and then refold the fabric strip. Top stitch along the top of each of the pockets, about ⅛" (3mm) away from each fold. Tack (baste) the side edges to hold the folded pockets firmly. Trim the pocket strip to 4½" (11.4cm) in height, trimming only from the top of the strip. Make a second set of credit card pockets in the same way, reusing the freezer paper template.

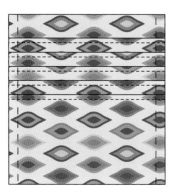

4   Make the coin pocket and flap next. Cut a rectangle of fabric for the pocket, 4½" x 7½" (11.4 x 19cm). Cut a piece the same size from the medium interfacing and iron to the back of the fabric (see Techniques, page 22). Fold the pocket piece in half (so it is 4½" x 3¾"/ 11.4 x 9.5cm), top stitch along the top (folded) edge and set aside.

5   ↓ Make the flap. Cut two pieces of fabric, 2½" x 4" (6.4 x 10.2cm), interface one of them using a piece of medium-weight interfacing, then place the two rectangles right sides together. Sew along the two short sides and the lower edge with a ¼" (6mm) seam. Now mark a dot 1" (2.5cm) up from the lower edge on both sides and 1" (2.5cm) in from the same corners. Draw lines joining the dots and then sew on the lines to chop off the corners.

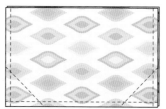

6   Trim the seam allowances down to ⅛" (3mm) and turn to the right side. Top stitch the three edges leaving the top edge open. Mark a dot in the centre of the flap, ½" (13mm) up from the bottom (sewn) edge. Use a stiletto to pierce a hole through the layers at the dot and apply the male part of the snap fastener and one cap. The cap should be on the top of the flap (right side) and the male part on the underside.

7   Cut a piece of contrast fabric 4¼" x 4½" (10.8 x 11.4cm) and layer the folded pocket on top, matching raw edges with the top, bottom and right hand side of the backing piece. Lay the flap on top, aligning the raw edge of the flap with the raw edge of the backing piece on the left. Mark a dot on the pocket where the snap fastener touches, remove the pocket and apply the female part of the snap fastener to the top and the cap on the back. Re-assemble the flap pocket and backing piece. Tack together around all four sides.

8 ↑ Assemble the lower section of the wallet. From contrast fabric cut two rectangles, each 4½" x 1½" (11.4 x 3.8cm). Lay out the pieces in order: credit card pockets, 1½" (3.8cm) rectangle, flap pocket plus backing, 1½" (3.8cm) rectangle and second set of credit card pockets. Sew each piece to the next with right sides together, using a ¼" (6mm) seam allowance. Press seam allowances towards the contrast strips. Top stitch either side of the left-hand contrast strip but do not top stitch the right hand one yet! Your finished strip should measure 4½" x 14" (11.4 x 35.5cm).

9 Cut a piece of contrast fabric, 5" x 14" (12.7 x 35.5cm), and a piece of medium-weight interfacing to the same size. Interface the back of the fabric. Place the contrast fabric and the lower wallet section right sides together and sew along the top edge with a ¼" (6mm) seam. Turn the contrast fabric to the back and match the side and bottom seams, press. This creates a ¼" (6mm) 'faux binding' effect on the front section. Top stitch the 'binding' very close to the seam. Set this section aside.

10 Make the zip pocket next. Cut a piece of fabric, 11" x 14" (28 x 35.5cm) and a piece of medium-weight interfacing to the same size. Interface the main pocket piece. Fold the pocket in half lengthways, wrong sides together, and press. Unfold.

11 → Cut a strip of contrast fabric, 2" x 8" (5 x 20.3cm). On the back of this strip draw a 'window' that is ½" (13mm) down from the top, ½" (13mm) deep and ½" (13mm) in from the sides. Pin this, right side down, to the wrong side of the interfaced pocket as shown, and sew around the window, on your drawn line. Cut through the window and into the corners and turn the facing through to the wrong side. Press well. Tack and then sew your zip into the window (see Techniques, page 28).

12 → Cut a piece of contrast fabric, 9½" x 5½" (24.1 x 14cm), and layer this behind the zip pocket, with the right side of the lining facing the wrong side of the zip. Tack in place, fold the pocket in half, and press. Top stitch the top edge and tack the side and lower edges together.

Make it yours...

```
If you have a lot of cards,
you could omit the middle
flap pocket and replace with
another card pocket, or omit
one of the credit card pockets
completely and replace with a
second flap pocket.

Make your wallet really
personalized with appliqués
added to the outer wallet
- just fuse and stitch
motifs onto the outer fabric
after you have ironed the
interfacing in place but
before you make up the wallet.
```

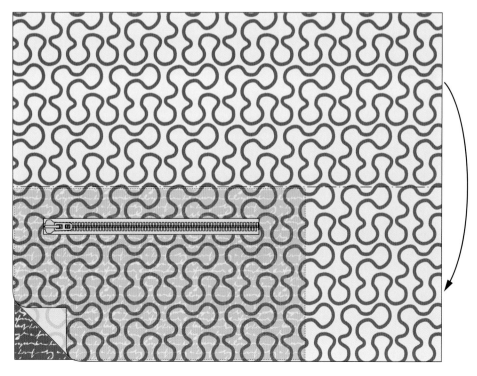

13 ↑ Cut a piece of contrast fabric, 6½" x 14" (16.5 x 35.5cm), and a piece of medium-weight interfacing the same size. Interface the fabric (see Techniques, page 22) and then layer the middle zip pocket on top and the credit card section on top of that as shown. Tack (baste) in place and then top stitch either side of the right hand contrast strip from bottom to top, creating pockets for notebook, pen and travel passes in the right hand section.

14 ↓ Make the fastening tab. Cut two pieces of contrast fabric, each 2" x 3" (5 x 7.6cm). Apply medium-weight interfacing to both and sew right sides together, leaving one short end open. 'Chop' the corners ¾" (19mm) from the ends, sewing on the drawn lines. Trim seam allowances and turn through. Press and top stitch around and then apply the male part of the snap fastener as before. Tack the tab to the centre of the right hand edge of the main wallet, cap facing up, raw edges aligned.

15 Cut a piece of fabric for the outside, 6½" x 14" (16.5 x 35.5cm), and a piece of heavy-weight interfacing. Interface the back of the fabric then layer the interfaced outer fabric with the inner wallet, right sides together. Sew all around the outside edge – use a shorter than normal stitch length and a ⅜" (10mm) seam allowance and leave a 4" (10.2cm) gap for turning. Trim the interfacing away very close to the seam allowance. Turn to the right side and press. Turn the raw edges of the gap in neatly and then top stitch around the outer edge of the wallet. It may be helpful to use a walking foot to do this.

16 Fold the wallet up and find the point where the male part of the snap fastener touches the back of the wallet. Mark a dot then apply the female part of the snap fastener, applying the snap only through the outer wallet and into the back pocket. The cap should be inside the back pocket.

PRODUCE BAGS

I love visiting food markets and whenever I'm travelling I always make a bee-line to wherever the locals shop for produce – my love of cooking is only second to my love for sewing! My produce bags are the perfect alternative to plastic bags and come in three useful sizes! Each size bag is made the same.

In this project we will make a cord casing, neaten seams and use cord locks.

FINISHED SIZES

	Height	Width
Small	11" (28cm)	7" (17.8cm)
Medium	12" (30cm)	11" (28cm)
Large	14" (35.5cm)	14" (35.5cm)

CUTTING

SMALL BAG
From the very light-weight cotton fabric cut:
• Main bag: 6½" x 25" (16.5 x 63.5cm) rectangle

From the contrast quilt weight cotton cut:
• Sides: two 1½" x 25" (3.8 x 63.5cm) strips
• Cord casings: two 2½" x 8½" (6.4 x 21.6cm) strips

MEDIUM BAG
From the very light-weight cotton fabric cut:
• Main bag: 8½" x 29" (21.6 x 73.7cm) rectangle

From the contrast quilt weight cotton cut:
• Sides: two 2½" x 29" (6.4 x 73.7cm) strips
• Cord casings: two 2½" x 12½" (6.4 x 31.8cm) strips

LARGE BAG
From the very light-weight cotton fabric cut:
• Main bag: 10½" x 33" (26.7 x 83.9cm) rectangle

From the contrast quilt weight cotton cut:
• Sides: two 3½" x 33" (8.9 x 83.9cm) strips
• Cord casings: two 2½" x 16½" (6.4 x 42cm) strips

Gather your supplies! You will need…

• Fabric

  Front and back: 29½" (0.75m) very light-weight but firmly woven fine cotton fabric –butter muslin, cheesecloth or cotton voile all work well (this will be enough to make all three bags)

  Sides and cord casing: one fat quarter per bag

• 3¼yd (3m) Roman blind cord (this will be enough to make all three bags)

• Lightweight plastic spring loaded cord lock

• Thread to match your fabrics

I used a variety of Ikat-style fabrics for the bag sides and cord casing – any quilt-weight cotton would be perfect here!

Make it yours...

Increase or decrease the size of the light-weight cotton panels and accent strips to create larger or smaller bags.

Make the whole bag from quilt-weight fabric for pyjamas or reusable gift bags or make the whole bag from very light-weight cotton and use for laundering fine lingerie in the washing machine.

LET'S MAKE THE BAG!

1 Sew the contrast strips to either side of the main bag panel. Press seam allowances towards the contrast strips and then top stitch ⅛" (3mm) inside the contrast strip to accent the strip but also to keep the seam allowance tidy and to prevent fraying.

2 On the main bag panel, turn a double ½" (13mm) hem at each of the short raw ends, press and then top stitch these two hems. Top stitch very close to the upper fold and also near to the bottom of the hem, creating two lines of stitching.

3 → Fold your cord casing strips in half lengthwise, wrong sides together, and gently finger press to form a crease and then unfold. Turn the long raw edges in towards the centre fold, wrong sides together again, and press to create a strip with two neatened long edges. Turn a double ½" (13mm) hem at each short end and stitch. Lay one of the neatened casings, centred, about 1" (2.5cm) down from one of the short ends of the main bag on the right side, and pin in place. Sew along the long edges to attach the casing to the bag. You want to sew pretty close to the edge of the casing, ⅛" (3mm) is perfect! Repeat with the second casing at the other end of the bag panel.

4 Fold the main bag panel in half, right sides together, bringing the two short ends together. Pin the side seams and sew these side seams using a ¼" (6mm) seam allowance and then neaten the raw edges of your seams with a zig zag or overlocking stitch.

5 Trim away the bottom corners of the bag as follows. For the small bag, trim away a ¾" (19mm) square, for the medium bag a 1½" (3.8cm) square and for the large bag a 2½" (6.4cm) square. Bring the side seams to meet the folded bottom edge to 'box' the corners. Sew the corners with a ¼" (6mm) seam allowance and then overlock or zig zag the raw edge of your seams to neaten (see Techniques, page 36).

6 Turn the bag to the right side. At either side, at the top, turn the seams to one side and stitch about 1" (2.5cm) through all layers to hold the seam allowance flat and neat.

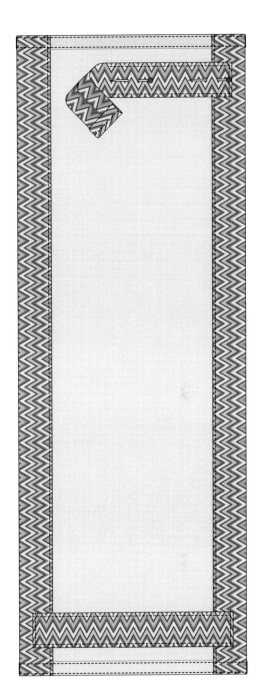

7 Cut a length of cord as follows: small 26" (66cm), medium 38" (96.5cm) and large 42" (106.7cm).

8 Thread the cord through the cord casing. Push the button down on the spring loaded cord lock and pass the two ends of the cord through the hole. Release the button to 'lock' in place. Knot the ends of the cord neatly.

EXPANDING SHOPPING BAG

I love a 'bag for life' when I'm doing my grocery shop but I'd much rather it matched my outfit! My expanding shopping bag folds away into a tiny bundle and is easy to pop into a pocket or bag for an impromptu trip to the market.

In this project we will sew simple seams, finish raw edges, make simple handles and attach elastic and a button.

FINISHED SIZE

17" x 17" (43 x 43cm)

CUTTING

From the main fabric cut:
- Bottom of bag: two 14½" x 17½" (36.8 x 44.5cm) rectangles, landscape
- Handle lining: two 2" x 16" (5 x 40.6cm) strips

Cut two handle lining pieces from interfacing and fuse to the wrong side of the handle lining pieces (see Techniques, page 22).

From the contrast fabric cut:
- Top of bag: two 3½" x 17½" (8.9 x 44.5cm) rectangles, landscape
- Handles: two 2" x 16" (5 x 40.6cm) strips

Gather your supplies! You will need…

- Fabric

  Main fabric: 19¾in (0.5m)

  Contrast fabric: 9¾in (0.25m)

- Medium-weight fusible interfacing: 1½" x 32" (3.8 x 81.3cm)

- Narrow elastic: 6" (15.2cm)

- A large button or toggle

- Thread to match your fabrics

I used some Ikat-style cotton prints as the main fabric and a navy print for the contrast fabric.

Make it yours...

You can make this bag out of just one fabric if you wish, but you'll still need that top strip to be added as a separate piece so that you can sandwich the elastic in the seam.

Add a wrist strap to the bag approximately 1" (2.5cm) to one side of the elastic loop. Make the wrist strap from a 2" (5cm) wide piece of interfaced fabric, folded into the centre and then folded in half and top stitched. It will need to be approximately 12–14" (30.5–35.5cm) in length to comfortably fit over your wrist when the bag is folded away.

LET'S MAKE THE BAG!

1 ↓ Take one of the main bag pieces and find and mark the centre, along the top edge. Fold the elastic in half and tack (baste) the two raw ends of the elastic in place at the centre mark, on the right side of the fabric, making a downward facing loop. The ends of the elastic should be side by side, just touching, rather than overlapping.

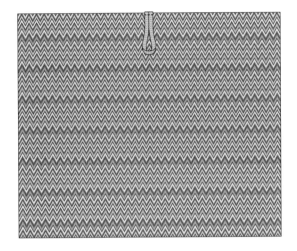

2 ↓ Pin one of the contrast top strips to the top of the bag panel, right sides together, sandwiching the elastic. Sew the pieces together using a ¼" (6mm) seam allowance. Overlock or zig zag the seam allowance to neaten. Press the seam allowance towards the contrast strip and top stitch ⅛" (3mm) from the seam. Make the back of the bag in the same way, omitting the elastic.

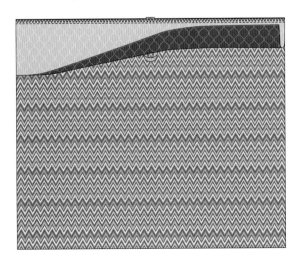

3 Make the bag handles. Sew one outer and one interfaced lining strip right sides together, leaving one short end open. Turn through to the right side and press. Top stitch along either long edge. Make the second handle in the same way.

4 Position each of the raw ends of one of the handles 5" (12.7cm) in from either outer edge of the bag front, making a loop shape, with the lining strip facing up towards you and with the handle loop pointing down. Tack in place, and repeat with the bag back.

5 Hem the bag top. On both front and back pieces, turn a ¼" (6mm) hem towards the wrong side, along the top of the bag, turning the handles back, too.

6 Turn another ¼" (6mm) hem back, press, and then turn the handles back up the right way and pin in place. Top stitch at the very top of the bag and just less than ¼" (6mm) away from this line, securing the top hem and handles in place.

7 Pin the front and back panels, right sides together, carefully matching the side and bottom edges and the seam where the contrast panel meets the main bag. Sew the side and bottom seams with a ⅜" (10mm) seam allowance and then overlock or zig zag stitch the raw edges to neaten them.

8 Turn the bag to the right side and press. Turn the side seam allowances towards one side and top stitch them in place to keep the top edge of the bag looking really neat.

9 Sew a button in place directly above the elastic loop, right in the centre of the contrast strip (see main photograph for placement).

To fold your bag away, lay it face down (elastic and button facing down) on a flat surface, turn the side thirds in and overlap them, turn the handles down and then lift the bottom edge up enough to cover at least half of the handles. From the bottom edge, roll the bag up fairly tightly and then pull the loop of elastic around the bundle and secure it over the button.

A DAY AT THE BEACH

Whether you go for pristine white sand, rocky crags and pebbles or a rugged coastal walk there really is nothing like spending a day at the beach. I love to look out at the water and imagine all the possibilities that lay beyond the horizon and I'm always inspired to make things for my trips!

My splash proof beach bag is a simple cylinder bag reminiscent of the sports bags I had as a child – lots of space inside for swim kit, towels, jelly shoes and sunhats, and all within a waterproof lining. There's even a waterproof zipped pocket on the front of the bag to keep your holiday novel safe and dry!

For more leisurely days take my convertible tote 'n' towel – a useful and roomy tote that magically opens out into a huge beach towel, with very handy mesh pockets inside to house sunglasses, magazines, sun protection and beach shoes. There's even a little bonus pillow to make lazing on the beach even more comfortable!

If looking stylish and walking around the marina are more your bag, you'll love my essential hobo bag – its chic curves and roomy interior make it fashionable (as well as useful)!

CONVERTIBLE TOTE 'N' TOWEL

A lovely roomy tote bag would be just the thing to carry your towel to the beach, but what if the tote opened out into a gorgeous comfortable towel, and what if there were useful mesh pockets inside the bag to hold sunscreen, books, sunglasses and a packed lunch too? Wish no more, grab some fabrics and make my expandable tote 'n' towel!

We'll be doing a bit of easy patchwork, sewing with mesh fabrics and waffle towelling and also inserting a long zip around a corner.

FINISHED SIZES

Finished bag (folded): 17" x 17" (43 x 43cm)
Towelling area (opened out): 53" x 59" (134 x 150cm), approx

CUTTING

From the main fabric cut:
- Top of outer bag: 10½" x 34½" (26.7 x 87.6cm) rectangle, landscape

From the accent fabric cut:
- Accent stripe on outer bag: 1½" x 34½" (3.8 x 87.6cm) strip
- Binding for internal mesh pockets: 2½" x 36" (6.4 x 91.4cm) strip

From the piecing fabric cut:
- Eight 2½" x 6½" (6.4 x 16.5cm) rectangles from fabric 1
- Nine 2½" x 6½" (6.4 x 16.5cm) rectangles from fabric 2

From the lining fabric cut:
- Bag lining: 17½" x 34½" (44.5 x 87.6cm) rectangle
- Towel backing: 54" x 60" (137.2 x 152.4cm) rectangle

LET'S MAKE THE BAG!

1 Start with the patchwork. I call this 'piano keys' because of the light and dark fabric placement, but you could use an assortment of similar tones or even one strip of fabric 6½" x 34½" (16.5 x 87.6cm) instead. Arrange your 2½" x 6½" (6.4 x 16.5cm) rectangles in a row – I alternated white and red. Flip two adjacent rectangles right sides together and sew down one long edge with a ¼" (6mm) seam allowance. Open up the sewn fabrics and add your next rectangle in the same way. Keep going until all of the rectangles are sewn together and then press seam allowances towards the darker fabrics. Check that your seam allowance is accurate and that your finished panel measures 6½" x 34½" (16.5 x 87.6cm).

2 Sew your 1½" x 34½" (3.8 x 87.6cm) accent strip to the top edge of your patchwork panel, using a ¼" (6mm) seam allowance. Press the seam allowance towards the accent strip and then sew the main 10½" x 34½" (26.7 x 87.6cm) bag panel to the accent strip. Use a ¼" (6mm) seam allowance, and if your fabric is directional, like mine, make sure you sew it on the right way up!

3 ↓ Layer your outer bag panel on top of the piece of quilt batting (wadding), which is a few inches bigger on all sides. With the right side of your panel facing up, use quilt tacking (basting) spray or curved safety pins to hold the layers together.

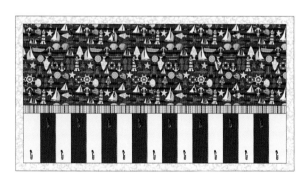

4 ↓ Quilt the bag panel as desired. I quilted straight lines either side of the piano key patchwork, along the seams of the accent strip and 'wavy' lines sewn randomly through the main panel. Also sew around the very edge of your bag panel, about ⅛" (3mm) in from the raw edge, then trim the wadding even with the bag top.

5 ↓ Pin the zip to the main bag panel. Undo the zip down to the last 1" (2.5cm). You can over-sew at the very end of the zip if you're nervous of pulling the zip pull right off! Start in the middle of your middle 'piano key' with the zip pull facing down with about 3" (7.6cm) of zip plus the zip pull hanging off the end. Make sure the zip teeth are facing inwards and the zip tape is even with the raw edge of your pieced panel.

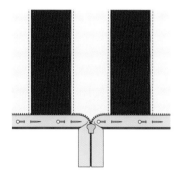

6 ↓ Pin the zip along the edge of the panel, keeping the zip tape against the raw edge. When you get to a corner, allow the zip to curve around it – snip into the zip tape a little with sharp scissors to help it bend if you find this easier. Continue to pin the zip up the side of the bag panel and when you get to the top corner fold the zip back and off at a 45-degree angle, leaving a little 'tail'.

7 Repeat on the other side of the bag with the other half of the zip. Tack (baste) the zip in place and remove the pins.

8 Make the bag lining. Start with the mesh pockets. Grab your pocket binding, and fold the 2½" (6.4cm) strip in half down the whole length, then unfold and turn the long raw edges in towards the centre fold. Press, and then refold the strip along the original centre fold to create a neat folded strip of binding. Use this strip to completely cover the raw top edge of the mesh fabric, pin it in place and then top stitch the lower edge of the binding, making sure that your stitches catch the binding in place on both sides. A walking foot is useful here to feed the mesh fabric through evenly. Be careful not to stretch the mesh fabric as you are sewing it!

9 ↓ Layer this bound mesh panel on top of your 17½" x 34½" (87.6 x 44.5cm) lining piece, lower raw edges aligned. Have the right side of your lining facing up and the right side of the mesh pocket facing up. Tack the pocket in place, then subdivide the pocket into four equal pockets by creasing a line at the centre and then at equidistant points either side. Sew through the mesh pocket into the lining at these points to divide up the pocket. Change the size of each individual pocket, if you prefer.

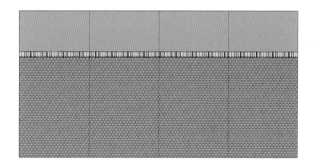

10 Layer the bag lining and main bag panel, right sides together, making sure that the bottom raw edge of the mesh pocket is at the bottom of the bag, lined up with the piano keys. Pin either side of the start of the zip, leaving a 1" (2.5cm) gap (you'll pull the zip pull back through this gap after you've finished sewing) and continue pinning all around the lower edge and the sides. Leave the top un-pinned and un-sewn at this stage.

11 Starting at the top of the bag, sew down one side, around the corner and finish sewing ½" (13mm) away from the zip pull. Reinforce your sewing at the point. Repeat the process on the other side of the bag, sewing from the top down to ½" (13mm) away from the zip pull. Turn your bag to the right side, pull the extra 3" (7.6cm) of zip and zip pull through the little gap you left, then thread the extra zip back into the gap, leaving the zip pull exposed. Press carefully and then top stitch around the side and bottom edges. You will not be able to sew over the very middle, right near the zip pull. As before, just reinforce stitch ½" (13mm) either side. You can hand sew the little gap if you wish.

12 ↓ Cut the webbing for the handles into two 33" (83.8cm) pieces. Place the edges of the handles 4" (10.2cm) in from the outer edges of the bag and 4" (10.2cm) in from the centre line, as shown. Tack in place.

13 ↓ Make the lined towel. Lay your waffle towelling panel down, with a short side at the top and the right side facing up. Place your opened bag with the mesh pocket against the towelling and the top raw edge of the bag aligned with the raw edge of the towelling, handles facing down. Cover this with the large lining panel, right side down and pin in place all around the top edge. Also pin the side and bottom edges together. Leave a 10" (25.4cm) gap at the bottom of the towel/lining for turning later. Sew all around the towel/lining, leaving the gap at the bottom un-sewn. Sew across the top edge too, joining your towel and lining to the bag. Use a ½" (13mm) seam

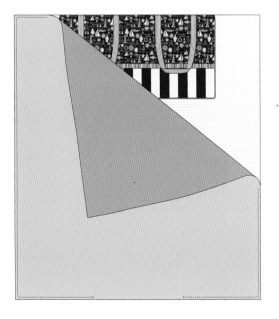

allowance. Turn though to the right side, push the corners out and press carefully.

14 ↓ Bring the open edges of your towel/lining together and pin. Pin around the entire towel and the edge, which joins it to the bag too. Top stitch all around the towel to close the opening and create a neat finished edge.

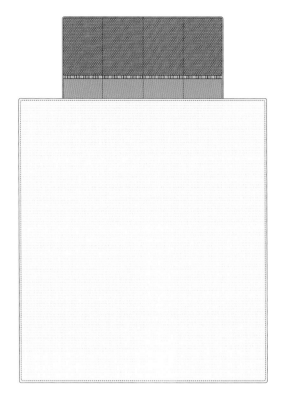

Make it yours...

I've made a little pillow for extra comfort at the beach. Cut two pieces of waterproof fabric each 12½″ x 15½″ (31.8 x 39.4cm). Sew all around, leaving a gap for turning. Fill with fibrefill and close the opening. Next make an outer cover. I used waffle towel on one side and patched some co-ordinating fabrics for the other side. I added a zip at the side and inserted the waterproof pillow inside!

The patchwork is optional — you could use a border print here to do the work for you, or add appliqué to a plain panel.

Use the same principles to make a pint-sized version for children — I'm very democratic when it comes to everyone doing their share of the carrying and children do love a bag!

Add extra pockets to the outer bag for greater functionality — add patch pockets to the outside of the outer bag after quilting and trimming.

SPLASH PROOF BEACH BAG

Whether you're heading to the beach for a swim or prefer relaxing and reading a novel, my splash proof beach bag is the perfect way to transport everything you need. The bag is lined with waterproof material, keeping everything safe, but there's also a separate waterproof zipped pocket to keep cash, books and keys safe from wet towels and swimming kit.

In this project we will sew gentle curves, use large metal eyelets and sew a 'letterbox' zip and pocket.

FINISHED SIZES

17" (43cm) x 10" (25.4cm)

CUTTING

From the main bag fabric cut:
• One 15½" x 35½" (39.4 x 90.2cm) rectangle, landscape
Cut the same size piece of medium-weight fusible interfacing and iron to the wrong side of the rectangle (see Techniques, page 22).

From the bottom fabric cut:
• One 5" x 35½" (12.7 x 90.2cm) strip
• Loops: two 4" x 5" (10.2 x 12.7cm) rectangles
Interface the small rectangles with medium-weight fusible interfacing (see Techniques, page 22).

From the base fabric cut:
• One 11" (28cm) diameter circle

From the waterproof fabric cut:
• Main bag lining: one 20" x 35½" (50.8 x 90.2cm) rectangle
• Internal zipped pocket: two 12" x 13" (30 x 33cm) rectangles
• Base: one 11" (28cm) diameter circle

From the fusible foam cut:
• One 11" (28cm) diameter circle
• One 5½" x 35½"(14 x 90.2cm) strip

Gather your supplies! You will need…

• Fabric

  Main bag: 19¾" (0.5m)

  Bottom of bag: one long quarter

  Base: one fat quarter

  Contrast/accent fabric: one 1" x 35½" (2.5 x 90.2cm) strip

  Waterproof fabric for lining and pocket: 29½" (0.75m)

• Fusible foam (such as Bosal In-R-Form): 19¾" (0.5m)

• Medium-weight fusible interfacing: 43" (110cm)

• One 12" (30cm) zip

• Eight ½" (14mm) eyelets and washers

• ¼–½" (10–12mm) cord: 2¼yd (2m)

• Thread to match your fabrics

• Wonder clips

I used a cotton print with coastal houses, lighthouses and boats for the main bag, a print with lobsters, lighthouses and sailing boats for the feature fabric at the bottom, a navy script print for the base (you can also use the same fabric here that you used for the top of the bag), a turquoise sun print for the contrast/accent fabric, and light grey waterproof fabric for my waterproof lining. You can buy waterproof fabric in all sorts of colours and prints but you could also repurpose a shower curtain here if you like! I used a turquoise zip to match my accent fabric and added a second zip pull. I used Prym silver eyelets and a navy blue cord.

LET'S MAKE THE BAG!

1 Start by making the bottom of the bag. Sew the 1" (2.5cm) contrast strip to the top of the 5" (12.7cm) base strip using a ¼" (6mm) seam allowance. Press the seam allowance towards the contrast strip then fuse this section to the 5½" (14cm) strip of fusible foam, matching all edges carefully. Top stitch along the seam joining the contrast strip and the base.

2 ↓ On one of the internal pocket pieces, measure 1½" (3.8cm) down from the top (12"/30cm) edge and draw a line across the fabric. Draw a second line ½" (13mm) down from this and then measure 1" (2.5cm) in from the sides and draw lines to create a rectangular 'letterbox' shape. Pin this marked pocket piece to the right side of your upper bag fabric, 4" (10.2cm) down from the top edge, centred and with the letterbox facing up. Sew around the 'letterbox' with a slightly shorter than usual stitch length.

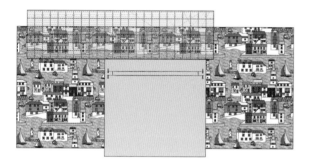

3 ↓ Carefully cut through the centre of the letterbox, right down the centre, stopping ¼" (6mm) from either end of the marked shape. Clip into the corners, then turn the pocket piece through the opening, just like you're posting a letter! Pull the pocket piece through to the wrong side, and finger press the edges of the letterbox opening really neatly.

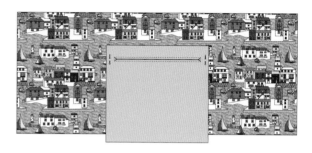

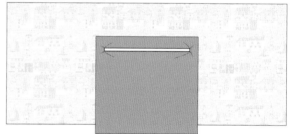

4 ↓ Centre your zip behind the opening, making sure that the zip pull is facing up and is within the opening. Pin and tack (baste) the zip in place, then machine sew from the right side using a zip foot and sewing very close to the edge of the letterbox opening.

5 ↓ From the wrong side, pin the second pocket piece to the first, matching all edges and being careful to pin pocket to pocket only. Don't pin the pocket to the bag front! Now sew all around the pinned pocket pieces using a ¼" (6mm) seam allowance. Test your pocket before proceeding!

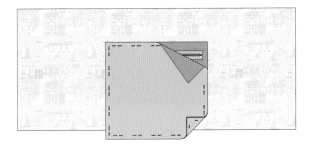

6 ↓ Sew the top of the bag to the bottom section using a ¼" (6mm) seam allowance and press the seam allowance towards the main bag piece. Top stitch close to this seam. Fold the main bag piece right sides together, matching the side seams. Pin then sew the side seam using a ½" (13mm) seam allowance. Press this seam allowance open and then turn the bag to the right side. Find the four quarter points on the bottom of the main bag and mark with pins. If it was a clockface, mark pins at 12, 3, 6 and 9 o'clock. Start with the centre back seam at 12 o'clock.

7 ↓ Take the two interfaced loop rectangles and fold each one in half lengthwise, right sides together (so they end up at 2" x 5"/5 x 12.7cm). Sew the side seam at ¼" (6mm). Turn to the right side, centre the long seam and press, then top stitch both long edges. Fold each in half and pin one each side of the centre back seam, raw edges of the loops aligned with the lower raw edge of the bottom of the bag. Tack (baste) in place.

8 ↓ Fuse the base circle of fabric to the circle of In-R-Form and find the quarter points around the outside edge as before – at 12/3/6 and 9 o'clock. Mark these points with pins, then clip the base circle to the bottom of the main bag, right sides together, using wonder clips and matching the quarter points on the bottom of the bag with the quarter points marked on base circle. Add extra clips between these four points.

9 Sew around the base of the bag using a ½" (13mm) seam allowance. Turn the bag to the right side and press.

10 Make the waterproof lining by folding the main bag piece in half, right sides together, and sewing the side seam, using a ½" (13mm) seam allowance. Mark the quarter points as before and do the same with the base circle. Clip the sections together and sew the base circle to the main piece using a ½" (13mm) seam allowance. Leave the lining wrong side out.

11 Drop the lining into the main bag, wrong sides touching, and match the upper raw edges. The lining is very slightly shorter to ensure a good fit. Pin and tack the lining in place. Turn a ½" (13mm) hem under and press. Be careful that your iron doesn't touch the waterproof fabric or it will melt! Then turn a second 1½" (3.8cm) hem and pin. Sew around the hem by machine.

12 Mark dots for the eyelets around the top of the bag. You want to place an eyelet 1" (2.5cm) or so either side of the centre back seam and then space the remaining 6 eyelets evenly around the top. Attach the eyelets following the manufacturer's instructions (see Techniques, page 39).

13 Thread your cord through the eyelets, starting and finishing either side of the centre back seam. Thread the cord through the loops at the base and knot them neatly. You could add a cord 'pocket' to cover the ends if you wanted to (see picnic blanket instructions, page 102).

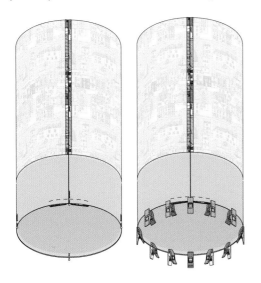

ESSENTIAL HOBO BAG

Here's a bag you'll make time and time again. Simple, stylish and roomy, its slouchy, relaxed style makes it perfect for a casual day at the beach, but stylish enough to take for lunch at the marina!

In this project we will use paper pattern pieces, make a decorative appliquéd bag base, sew curved seams and make a tied shoulder strap.

FINISHED SIZES

13" x 18" x 3½" (33 x 46 x 9cm), approx

CUTTING

From the main body fabric cut:
- Two of Beach Hobo Bag Pattern Piece A (see pull-out pattern sheet)
  Cut notches as marked on the pattern for box pleats.

From the lower bag trim/button loop fabric cut:
- Two of Bag Pattern Piece B (see pattern sheet)
- Button loop: one 2½" x 6½" (6.4 x 16.5cm) rectangle

From the gusset/shoulder straps fabric cut:
- Four 4" x 42" (10.2 x 106.7cm) strips

From the lining fabric cut:
- Two of Bag Pattern A + B cut as a single piece (see pull-out pattern sheet)
  Cut notches as marked on the pattern for box pleats.
- Gusset and shoulder straps: four 4" x 42" (10.2 x 106.7cm) strips

Cut 4" (10.2cm) strips from the interfacing and interface two of the 4" x 42" (10.2 x 106.7cm) strips of lining fabric for the shoulder straps (see Techniques, page 22).

From the quilt wadding (batting) cut:
- Two of Bag Pattern Piece A (see pattern sheet)
- Gusset: one 4" x 48" (10.2 x 122cm) strip

Gather your supplies! You will need...

- Fabric

  Main body of the bag A: 19¾in (0.5m)

  Lower bag trim B and button loop: 9¾in (0.25m)

  Gusset and shoulder straps: 19¾in (0.5m)

  Lining: 39½" (1m)

- Medium-weight fusible interfacing: 19¾in (0.5m)

- Quilt wadding (batting): a crib-sized piece, 40" x 60" (102 x 152cm), is plenty, or use offcuts

- One large button

- Threads to match your fabrics and button

- 505 quilt tacking (basting) spray

I used a cotton print featuring coastal cottages, lighthouses and yachts for the main body of the bag A, a red batik for the lower bag trim B and button loop, a multi-coloured nautical stripe for the gusset and shoulder straps and a navy script print for the lining.

LET'S MAKE THE BAG!

1   Layer one main fabric body piece A with a corresponding piece of quilt wadding (batting) and spray tack (baste) the wadding to the wrong side of your fabric. Prepare both main body A pieces in the same way.

2   ↓ Turn the inner edge of the contrast trim B pieces under by ¼" (6mm) and press. Clip inner curves as necessary to get a smooth finish. Layer these pieces on top of the main bag panels, aligning lower raw edges and pin in place. Top stitch the turned edge down onto the main bag piece and batting (wadding) and also tack around the lower edge ⅛" (3mm) in from the raw edge, to hold everything together.

3   ↓ Make the box pleats at the top of the bag by bringing each outer notched edge in to meet the centre notch. Pin then tack in place. Repeat this on both outer bag panels.

4 ↓ Sew two of the outer bag gusset fabric pieces together to make a strip that is 4" x 84" (10.2 x 213cm). This is much longer than we need, so trim the strip to 4" x 48" (10.2 x 122cm), centring the seam so that it can be hidden under the bag. Layer this gusset fabric on top of the strip of quilt wadding (batting), right side facing up, and spray tack the layers together. The gusset strip is still slightly longer than is necessary. Pin it around the sides and lower edges of one of the main bag pieces, right sides together (remember there will be excess gusset fabric at the end to trim off). Sew the gusset to the main bag panel with a ⅜" (10mm) seam. Trim the top edges level with the bag panel, then repeat on the other side. Press the seam allowances towards the gusset. Turn the main bag right side out.

5 Make the button loop by pressing the 2½" x 6½" (6.4 x 16.5cm) strip in half lengthwise, right sides out. Open up the strip and turn the long raw edges inwards to the centre crease and press, then refold the strip in half along the original crease. Top stitch down the long edges on both sides. Fold the strip in half to create a loop and tack in place over the box pleat on the back of the bag, loop pointing down, raw edges aligned.

6 Make the lining of the bag in a similar way to the outer bag. There is no lower contrast trim to add this time, but make the box pleats as before. Sew two of the 4" x 42" (10.2 x 106.7cm) lining gusset strips together and trim to 48" (122cm), centring the seam. Sew the lining gusset to the main lining bag pieces as before, but this time leave a 6" (15.2cm) gap in one of the seams at the bottom edge for turning the bag later. Leave the lining wrong side out.

```
Make it yours...

Add patch (slip) pockets to
the inside of your lining for
greater storage possibilities
and use waterproof lining
fabric for the inside of the
bag to make a very useful baby
changing bag.
```

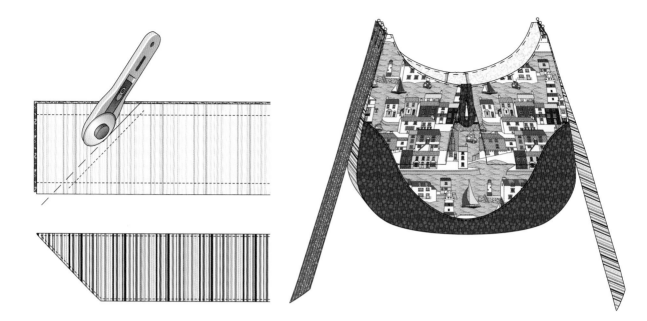

7 ↑ Make the shoulder straps. Place one interfaced lining strap piece right sides together with an outer fabric strap piece. Sew along both long edges with a ⅜" (10mm) seam allowance. Trim one of the lower (short) edges at a 45-degree angle and then sew this edge, with a ⅜" (10mm) seam allowance as before, to create a pointed end. Leave the other short edge open. Turn to the right side and push the pointed end out. Flatten the whole strap neatly, press then topstitch around the edges, ⅛" (3mm) in. Make a second shoulder strap in exactly the same way.

8 ↑ Pin one shoulder strap (at the raw open end) to the top of the gusset on the outer bag. Tack in place. Repeat with the second shoulder strap on the other side. Make sure both are tacked outer fabric to outer fabric (lining fabric on the shoulder strap facing up). Tuck the shoulder straps down out of the way. Also pin or tuck the button loop down out of the way.

9 Place the outer bag inside the lining, right side of the outer bag touching the right side of the lining. Match and pin the top edge of the bag and lining. Sew all around the top of the bag with a ⅜" (10mm) seam allowance. Turn the bag to the right side, press and then close the opening in the lining by hand or machine.

10 Press and pin the upper edge of the bag, smoothing the lining down neatly. Top stitch around the top of the bag, ⅛" (3mm) in from the edge. Sew your button on the front of the bag, right in the middle of the front box pleat. Tie the two shoulder straps together in the middle, with a large knot. Adjust the length to suit your frame.

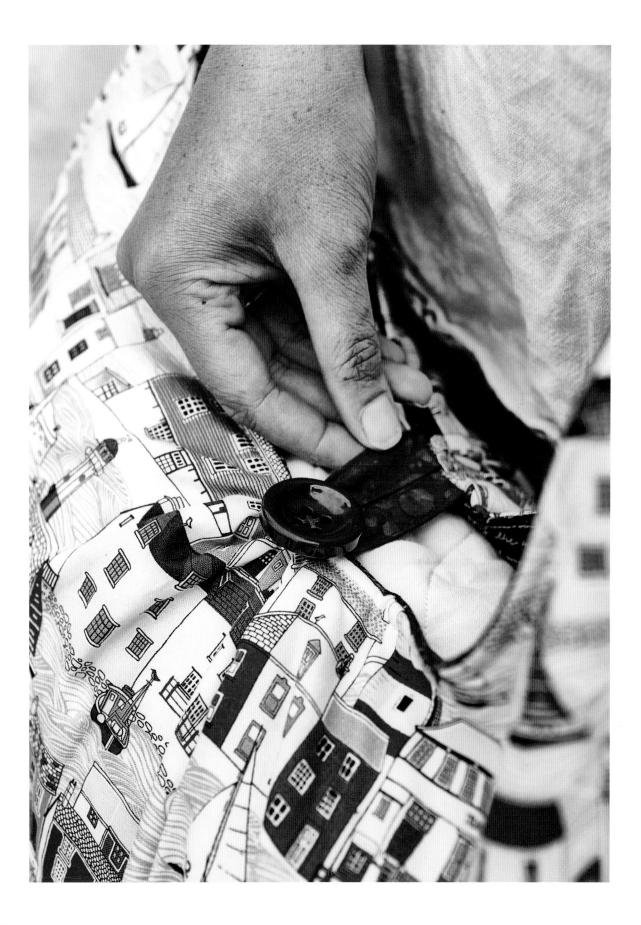

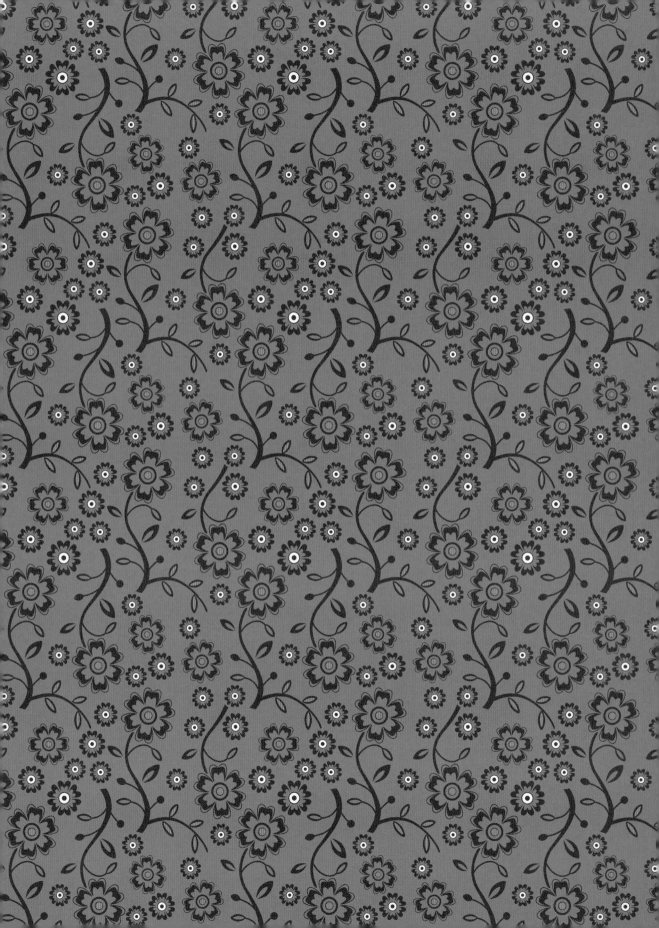

A PICNIC BY THE LAKE

I've always loved eating outside... there's something about throwing down a blanket and eating food in the open air that turns a sandwich and a bottle of water into an impromptu feast! High days and holidays can be made more special with my picnic and outdoor dining bags.

There are simple insulated lunch bags, which make a perfect 'grab and go' lunch possible for school, work or just a walk down to the park. My bottle carrier allows you to stay hydrated on long walks and helps to spread the weight of the bottles and free up hands. There's even a handy pocket for snacks – healthy ones of course!

My picnic blanket bag turns the necessity for a blanket into an opportunity for another gorgeous bag – this time a simple drawstring holdall with rucksack-style shoulder straps. Pop pillows inside or games to play after lunch.

Finally, my picnic bag is the ultimate carrier for everything you'll need for the feast. Pockets galore ensure there's space for wine and water, plates, cutlery and napkins and, of course, all that lovely food!

INSULATED LUNCH BAGS

These nifty lunch bags are perfect for taking food to the office or school and they have a layer of heat reflective batting (wadding) inside them which will help to maintain the temperature of your food. They also fit beautifully inside my ultimate picnic bag making them perfect for alfresco dining.

In this project we will use heat reflective quilt batting (wadding) and make a closure using Velcro.

FINISHED SIZES

11" x 7" x 3½" (28 x 17.8 x 8.9cm)

CUTTING

From the main outer fabric cut:
Two 14" x 12" (35.5 x 30cm) rectangles, portrait

From the lining fabric cut:
Two 14" x 12" (35.5 x 30cm) rectangles, portrait

Gather your supplies! You will need...

- Fabric

  Main outer fabric: 19¾" (0.5m)

  Lining fabric: 19¾" (0.5m)

- Thermal insulating batting (wadding): two 12" x 14" (30 x 35.5cm) pieces

- Sew-able Velcro (make sure you have both parts!): 6" (15.2cm) piece

- 505 quilt tacking (basting) spray or curved safety pins

- Thread to match your fabrics

- Wonder clips

I used bright geometric and floral cotton fabrics for the main bags and solid navy cotton fabric for the linings.

LET'S MAKE THE BAG!

1   Layer one outer fabric rectangle on top of a piece of insulating batting (wadding), right side of your fabric facing up. Tack (baste) the layers together with quilt tacking (basting) spray or pin well with curved safety pins. Quilt the layers together if you wish or just tack around the outside edge, ⅛" (3mm) in from the raw edges. Remove safety pins if using. Repeat with the second outer piece.

2   ↓ Find the centre point of the outer rectangles at the top (short) edge and carefully pin one half of the Velcro down the centre. Top stitch the Velcro in place. Repeat with the other half of the Velcro on the other outer rectangle.

3   Place the two layered rectangles on top of each other, right sides together, Velcro attached, raw edges lined up. Pin the sides and the bottom edges. Sew the sides and the bottom edges with a ¼" (6mm) seam allowance.

4   ↓ Trim a 2" (5cm) square away from both bottom corners and then 'box' the bottom corners of the bag by bringing the cut edges together (see Techniques, page 36). Sew across the corners with a ¼" (6mm) seam allowance. Turn the bag to the right side.

5   Where you have boxed the corners of your bag, you'll see that the bag now has a more 3D shape. From the corners you've just made, pinch the edges of the bag together and pin or hold the pinched edges with wonder clips. Do this on the sides of your bag, as well as the front and back and also along the bottom. Top stitch along this fold, very close to the fold – ⅛" (3mm), no more – to really emphasize the box shape.

6   Make the lining for your lunch bag by pinning the two lining rectangles together, sewing the side and bottom seams and adding the box corners as on the outer bag. This time there's no Velcro. Leave a 4–5" (10–13cm) gap unsewn in one of the sides, about halfway down from the top.

7   Insert your outer bag into the lining, right sides together, and match up the top edges and side seams. Pin well then sew all around the top of your bag using a ⅜" (10mm) seam allowance.

8   Turn your bag to the right side, close the opening in the lining by hand or machine, then roll the lining down into the bag. Match the top edges and pin well, then top stitch all around the top edge of your bag.

To close the bag, simply push the sides in a little then roll the top down – the Velcro keeps everything securely held until you're ready for lunch!

Make it yours...

Instead of one fabric for the outside of the bag, why not use a 4¼" x 12" (10.8 x 30cm) piece of contrast fabric for the base of the outer bag and a 10¼" x 12" (26 x 30cm) piece of feature fabric for the top of the bag? You'll need one of each for the front of the bag and the same again for the back. Sew the pieces of fabric together and then proceed with the pattern.

I've also made these bags for carrying takeaway food home from the restaurant, but I've made them a little wider and deeper: 14" x 16" (35.5 x 40.6cm) panels with a 3" (7.6cm) square cut out of each lower corner.

PICNIC BAG

This is the perfect large bag for carrying a full picnic for four or more people, hugely roomy inside and with lots of pockets to keep everything safe and organized! Stylish and beautiful in your favourite print and solid combo, it is functional in the extreme. There are six pockets built into the lining to house cool blocks and on the outside there are a total of ten more pockets to hold everything from plates and cutlery to napkins and bottles of wine. The bag also features two sturdy carrying handles and a detachable and adjustable shoulder strap. This is a challenging make and will take time but the results are well worth the effort!

We will make an adjustable shoulder strap, pleated pockets, add bag feet and use an open-ended zip.

FINISHED SIZES

18" x 12" x 8" (45.7 x 30 x 20.3cm)

CUTTING

In this project we will cut and piece different sections of the bag one at a time to keep things organized.

Gather your supplies! You will need...

- Fabric

  Main fabric for outer bag: 59" (1.5m)

  Co-ordinating solid fabric for the outer bag, handles and shoulder strap: 59" (1.5m)

  Fabric for lining the main bag and the outer pockets: 59" (1.5m)

  Co-ordinating fabric for the lining pockets: 19¾" (0.5m)

  Co-ordinating fabric for the lining pocket tops: 19¾" (0.5m)

- 1" (2.5cm) webbing in a co-ordinating colour: 60" (152cm)

- Two 1½" (3.8cm) swivel clips

- Two 1½" (3.8cm) D-rings

- One 1½" (3.8cm) strap slider

- Four bag feet

- One 16" (40.6cm) open-ended zip in a co-ordinating colour

- Fusible foam (such as Bosal In-R-Form): 40" x 58" (100 x 147cm)

- Quilt batting (wadding): 15" x 24" (38.1 x 61cm)

- Medium-weight fusible interfacing: 16" (40.6cm)

- Thread to match your fabrics

I used bright geometric and floral cotton fabrics for the main bag and lining with a co-ordinating solid navy cotton fabric for the outer bag, handles and shoulder strap. I used the same solid cotton fabric that I used on the outside of the bag for the lining pocket tops.

LET'S MAKE THE BAG!

1 From the main outer fabric cut the main bag pieces. Front and back: two 12½" x 8½" (31.8 x 47cm) rectangles, landscape. Sides: two 12½" x 8½" (31.8 x 21.6cm) rectangles, portrait. Base: 8½" x 18½" (21.6 x 47cm) rectangle, landscape. Cut exactly the same number and sizes of pieces in fusible foam and fuse the foam to the back of the fabric pieces (see Basic Techniques, page 22).

2 On the foam side of the bag base mark a point 2" (5cm) in from each of the corners. Use very sharp scissors or a stiletto to make a small hole at each mark, then from the right side push the prongs of one of the bag feet through to the wrong side, open out the prongs and press down firmly. Repeat at each corner. Set the outer bag pieces to one side.

3 Make the pleated side pockets. From the main outer fabric, cut two 8½" x 11½" (21.6 x 29.2cm) rectangles, landscape. From the co-ordinating solid fabric, cut two 2½" x 11½" (6.4 x 29.2cm) rectangles, for the pocket tops. From the lining fabric, cut two 10½" x 11½" (26.7 x 29.2cm) rectangles.

4 ↓ Sew the pocket tops to the top of the main pocket pieces with ¼" (6mm) seam allowance. Press seam allowances towards the pocket tops. Place an outer pocket piece and a lining piece right sides together and sew the top seams using a ¼" (6mm) seam allowance. Turn to the right side and bring the lining and outer pieces neatly together. Press and then top stitch close to the seams on the pocket tops. Tack (baste) the side and bottom edges to keep them together. Make a second pocket in the same way.

5 ↓ At the bottom of the pockets find and mark the centre and also 1½" (3.8cm) either side of the centre mark. Bring these outer markings in to meet the centre mark, forming a pleat. Tack the pleat in place. Repeat on both side pockets and then tack the pocket in place on top of the main bag sides, aligning the lower raw edges.

7 ↓ On a piece of wadding (batting) lay a main outer pocket piece, right side of the pocket facing up, and then lay a piece of lining fabric on top of the outer pocket, wrong side facing up. Sew along the top edge only. Open the fabrics out and press back, covering the wadding with the lining and pressing the top edge neat and flat. Top stitch this top edge, then tack the sides and bottom edge to hold them neatly together. Make two plate pockets in this way and set aside.

6 Make the plate pockets. Cut two 10½" x 12½" (26.7 x 31.8cm) rectangles, landscape, from the main outer fabric, two more from the lining fabric and two more from the quilt wadding (batting).

8 Make the cutlery/napkin pockets. From the main outer fabric, cut two 4½" x 12½" (11.4 x 31.8cm) rectangles, landscape. From the co-ordinating solid fabric, cut two 2½" x 12½" (6.4 x 31.8cm) rectangles. From the lining fabric, cut two 6½" x 12½" (16.5 x 31.8cm) rectangles.

9 Sew the co-ordinating solid pocket tops to the main fabric pieces with ¼" (6mm) seam and press. Sew the main pocket to the lining at the top edge only, flip the lining back and press, then top stitch the pocket tops at top and bottom. Tack (baste) the side and bottom edges together. Make two in the same way.

10 Lay one cutlery pocket on top of a plate pocket and align the side and bottom edges. Tack the pockets together, then divide the cutlery pocket into three equal pockets, marking lines lightly with a fabric marking pen. Sew along these lines, through the cutlery pocket and into the plate pocket, to subdivide the outer pocket. Make two in the same way. Layer one of the plate/cutlery pocket combos on top of one of the main bag front/back pieces, centring the pockets. Tack in place. Repeat with the other pocket piece and the other main bag front/back piece.

11 ↓ Make the plate pocket closures. From the co-ordinating solid fabric, cut two 4½" x 12½" (11.4 x 31.8cm) rectangles, landscape. Cut two rectangles of medium-weight fusible interfacing to the same size. Interface the wrong side of the rectangles (see Techniques, page 22). Fold one rectangle in half lengthwise, right sides together and press. Sew along the top edge to make a tube, turn to the right side, centre the seam at the back and press. Top stitch along the lower edge about an ⅛" (3mm) in from the lower edge. Make a second pocket closure in the same way. Tack the pocket closure over the plate pockets, covering the plate pocket top by approximately 1" (2.5cm). Repeat for both pocket closures and then top stitch along the very top of the pocket closure, attaching it to the main bag at the same time. Repeat with the other pocket closure.

12 Make the bag handles. From the co-ordinating solid fabric, cut four 2" (5cm) strips, each 44" (111.8cm) in length. Cut two strips of medium-weight fusible interfacing to the same size, and interface two of the fabric strips (see Techniques, page 22).

13 Place one interfaced strip right side to right side with a fabric strip and sew around three sides with a ¼" (6mm) seam, leaving one short end open. Turn to the right side and press. Make two in the same way.

14 ↓ Lay one bag handle on the main bag piece, starting at the bottom edge and layering the inner handle edge ½" (13mm) over the tacked pocket edges. Repeat on the other side of the same pocket. Top stitch the handle in place on either side of the pocket. Sew a 'box' on the handle, at the top of the plate pocket to reinforce this 'stress' area (see Techniques, page 34). You can also top stitch the rest of the handle at this point. Repeat on the other main bag piece with the second handle.

15 Make the zipped bag top. From the main outer fabric, cut two 5" x 17½" (12.7 x 44.5cm) rectangles. Cut two more from the lining fabric and two from the fusible foam.

16 ↓ Open the zip out into two halves. Fuse one main fabric piece to a piece of fusible foam, right side of your fabric facing up. Lay one half of your zip on top, lining up the raw edge of the fabric with the zip tape, teeth facing inwards. The zip is shorter than the fabric/foam so make sure you centre the zip.

17 ↓ Pin and tack the zip in place, then layer your lining piece on top, sew around the short ends and the zip side using a zipper foot. Use a ½" (13mm) seam allowance at the ends and sew close to the zip.

18 ↓ Turn through to the right side, press and top stitch close to the zip and side seams. Repeat with the other pieces of fabric and foam and the other half of the zip. Be very careful to position the other half of the zip on the opposite side of the foam/fabric so that the two halves will meet in the middle! Set the bag top to one side.

19 Assemble the main bag using box bag technique (see page 36). Sew the main bag panels to the base, right sides together. Use a ⅜" (10mm) seam allowance and start and finish sewing ⅜" (10mm) from either end. Sew the bag sides to the base, right sides together, starting and finishing your seam ⅜" (10mm) in from the ends. Sew the four side seams, starting right at the top of the bag and finishing at the ⅜" (10mm) point at the bottom edge. Turn the bag to the right side. With right sides touching, tack the bag top pieces to either side of the main bag, centring the bag top carefully so that both halves line up.

20 Make the D-ring attachments and the shoulder strap. From the co-ordinating solid fabric cut two 2" (5cm) strips, each 60" (152.4cm) in length. Join two shorter strips, if necessary. Cut two strips of medium-weight fusible interfacing to the same size, and interface one of the fabric strips (see Techniques, page 22).

21 Layer the two strips of fabric right sides together and sew along the long edges and one short edge with a ¼" (6mm) seam allowance. Turn through to the right side and press. Pin a 60" (152.4cm) length of co-ordinating webbing to the shoulder strap, centring the webbing, and then top stitch the webbing in place. Trim the short closed end off and discard.

22 Cut two pieces off this strap, each 3" (7.6cm) long, for the D-ring attachments. Pass one piece through a D-ring, bring the raw edges together and tack (baste) in the centre of the bag side panel. Repeat with the other 3" (7.6cm) piece, the D-ring and the other end of the bag. Make sure the raw edges are aligned and the D-rings are hanging down. Use the remaining 54" (137.2cm) of strap to make the shoulder strap. Install the strap slider and the swivel clips (see Techniques, page 34) and then sew them in place. Leave the shoulder strap off the bag for the time being.

23 Make the bag lining and internal pockets. From the co-ordinating fabric, cut two 7" x 18½" (17.8 x 47cm) rectangles for the outside of the internal pockets. From the co-ordinating solid fabric, cut two 8" x 18½" (20.3 x 47cm) rectangles to line and edge the internal pockets. Apply fusible interfacing to these two rectangles (see Techniques, page 22).

24 Sew one internal pocket piece to one internal pocket lining, along the top edge, flip the lining back and bring the lower raw edges together. This will leave a contrast edge to the main pocket fabric. Press and top stitch this top edge. Make two in the same way.

25 From lining fabric, cut: two 12½" x 18½" (31.8 x 47cm) rectangles; two 8½" x 12½" (21.6 x 31.8cm) rectangles and one 8½" x 18½" (21.6 x 47cm) rectangle. Tack the pocket pieces to the two largest rectangles and subdivide into pockets. (I made mine to very generously fit my 'cold pack' blocks into.) And then make the lining up in the same way as the main outer bag. Use ½" (13mm) seam allowances and leave an 8" (20.3cm) gap in one of the bottom seams for turning the bag later. Leave the lining wrong side out.

26 Assemble the whole bag. Put the outer bag inside the lining, right sides touching. Make sure that you match side seams first, all raw edges, and ensure that the zip tops are tucked into the sides, as well as the D-rings. Sew all around the top of the bag with a ⅜" (10mm) seam allowance. Turn through to the right side, close the opening in the lining by hand or machine. Line up the outer bag and the lining edges very neatly and pin in place. Top stitch all around the top edge of the bag. Attach the shoulder strap.

```
Make it yours...

Make some quick and easy
matching napkins by cutting
15½" (39.4cm) squares of co-
ordinating fabric. Turn a
double ¼" (6mm) hem all around
the edges and stitch with
matching thread.
```

BOTTLE CARRIER

Worn on your shoulder or across your body, this is the perfect bottle carrier for hikes in the hills or a leisurely ramble round the lakes. The carrier is interlined with an insulating layer of wadding (batting), which helps to keep your cold drinks nicely chilled for refreshment on the go!

FINISHED SIZES

8" x 3" (20 x 7.5cm)

CUTTING

From the main outer fabric cut:
- Outer carrier: one 6¼" x 10" (15.9 x 25.4cm) rectangle, landscape
- Base: one 3½" (8.9cm) diameter circle
- Pocket: one 6" x 5" (15.2 x 12.7cm) rectangle

From the lining fabric cut:
- One 8" x 10" (20.3 x 25.4cm) rectangle
- One 3½" (8.9cm) diameter circle

LET'S MAKE THE BAG!

1 Cut two 3" (7.6cm) lengths of the webbing leaving a 50" (127cm) length for the shoulder strap. Slip one 3" (7.6cm) piece through a D-ring and tack (baste) the raw ends together. Make two.

2 Take the main outer rectangle and, along the top edge, mark a point 2¾" (7cm) in from each side and layer your D-ring loops here. Pin then sew in place, less than ¼" (6mm) from the raw edges.

3 Lay the contrast outer piece against the top edge, pin, then sew the contrast band on. Press it back and then layer the outer bag piece on top of the piece of quilt wadding (batting), right side uppermost. Pin or tack in place. Quilt the outer bag if you like – I quilted straight vertical lines – lifting the D-ring loops away as you quilt.

```
Make it yours...

This is a very easy bag to
adapt to fit your favourite
water bottle. Measure around
your bottle, loosely, and
add ½" (13mm) for the seam
allowance. Measure the height
of the bottle from base to top
and use that measurement for
the other dimension of your
rectangle. No need to add seam
allowance this time – we want
the bottle carrier to be a bit
shorter than the bottle. For
the base circle, draw around
the bottle base. If the bottle
narrows at the base, go with
the widest dimension and add
a ¼" (6mm) seam allowance all
around. You'll probably be
able to find a glass or mug
with the same(ish!) size base
to draw around (or use a set
of compasses).

Pockets can be made bigger to
house larger snacks or your
phone or left off altogether
but seriously, who doesn't
love a snack on a long walk?
```

4 Turn a double ¼" (6mm) hem at the top edge of the pocket piece, press, then sew this edge. Turn a single ¼" (6mm) hem along the sides and press, then make a pleat in the centre bottom of the pocket by marking the centre and bringing ½" (13mm) of fabric from either side in to meet the centre, creating a little inverted pleat. Tack and then turn a single ¼" (6mm) hem at the bottom of the pocket. Position the pocket on the front of the bottle carrier, within the space between the straps and around ¾" (19mm) up from the bottom. Sew the pocket in place.

5 Fold the outer bag in half, right sides together, and sew the side edge with a ¼" (6mm) seam allowance.

6 Layer the outer fabric base circle and the circle of wadding, right side of fabric facing up, and quilt as desired. You could quilt straight lines across the circle as I did or just an X through the centre.

7 Find the quarter points around the base of your carrier and mark with pins. Do the same with the base circle, then pin the base and bag, right sides together, matching up the quarter marks. Sew around the base with a ¼" (6mm) seam. Turn the carrier to the right side.

8 Make the lining by folding the lining rectangle in half, right sides together, and sewing the side seam, but this time leave a 3" (7.6cm) gap in the middle of the seam for turning. Sew the base into the lining as before.

9 Put your outer bag into the lining, right sides together, matching the centre seams and then pinning around the top of the bag. Sew with a ¼" (6mm) seam allowance.

10 Turn the bag through to the right side, sew up the gap in the lining and press the top edge. Top stitch by hand or machine, if desired.

11 Slip the raw ends of the shoulder strap through the D-rings and sew securely in place, sewing a cross for security (see Techniques, page 34).

PICNIC BLANKET BAG

Any picnic worth its salt should include lots of time sprawling in the sunshine on a beautiful blanket. What if this blanket could also transport toys and games for the picnic party and then make clearing up at the end a breeze? This isn't just possible, it's easy to achieve, with my picnic blanket bag! It's a simple sling-style bag with a drawstring cord to hold everything secure with rucksack-style shoulder straps for comfortably carrying games, toys or cushions to the picnic. Opened out, the bag transforms into a generous picnic blanket and is softly padded for comfort. When the picnic is done or (more likely!) the rain comes, throw everything into the centre of the blanket and pull up the drawstrings and you'll be on your way in minutes!

In this project we will make a simple patchwork quilt and make simple tabs and shoulder straps.

FINISHED SIZES

Diameter: 60" (152cm) when opened out

CUTTING

From the printed quilt-weight cotton fabrics:
- Cut each fabric into 6½" (16.5cm) wide strips and then cut rectangles from these strips. I've cut a variety of different lengths, from 7½" (19cm) to 21½" (54.6cm), but they are all 6½" (16.5cm) wide. You'll need lots, but it's a good idea to cut a bunch, arrange them on the floor and cut more as you need them – you'll need around 34 in total but I always like to cut extra so that I can play around with colour placement. You can always use the extras for a little pillow or cushion to go with your blanket bag.

→

Gather your supplies! You will need…

- Fabric

  For piecing the blanket I've used quilt-weight cotton fabrics – ten different fabrics in a variety of prints. 19¾" (0.5m) cuts of each fabric will give you plenty.

  Print fabric for cord tabs, rucksack-style straps and cord pocket: 19¾" (0.5m)

  Solid for cord tabs, binding and strap end covers: 39½" (1m)

  Blanket backing: 64" (162.6cm) square piece (join fabrics together to make a piece large enough)

- Quilt batting (wadding): 64" (162.6cm) square

- 1" (2.5cm) wide webbing: two 28" (71cm) pieces (for the rucksack-style straps)

- Cord (¼"/6mm wide minimum): 5½yd (5m)

- 505 quilt tacking (basting) spray

- Thread to match your fabrics

- 30" (76cm) piece of string

- Marking pen

I used a solid navy for two of the cord tabs, the strap end covers and the blanket binding. I also used a navy solid as a blanket backing. I used a purple print for the remaining two cord tabs, rucksack-style straps and cord pockets. I used a co-ordinating navy cord and navy webbing for the straps.

From the solid cut:

- Cord tabs: Two 2" x 42" (5 x 106.7cm) strips
- Strap end covers: Eight 3½" (8.9cm) squares
- Binding (for edge of blanket): Six 2½" x 42" (6.4 x 106.7cm) strips cut on the bias, joined together with diagonal seams (see Techniques, page 21)

From the print cut:

- Cord tabs: Two 2" x 42" (5 x 106.7cm) strips
- Rucksack-style straps: Four 2½" x 28" (6.4 x 71cm) strips
- Cord pocket: Two 2½" (6.4cm) squares

I used a variety of blue and purple quilt-weight prints for the patchwork, ten different ones in total.

LET'S MAKE THE BAG!

1 Arrange the 6½" (16.5cm) wide rectangles of piecing fabric on the floor in ten rows, staggering the joins to create an 'uneven brick wall' effect. Ten rows will give you a joined width of 60½" (153.7cm). You need 60½" (153.7cm) in length too, so add more rectangles until you have a piece large enough. Sew the 'bricks' together in long rows, using a ¼" (6mm) seam allowance and pressing the seam allowances one way. Once you have made ten rows, join the rows together and press the seams one way.

2 Layer this 'patchwork' with the wadding (batting) and backing fabric, with the wadding inside and the backing and patchwork either side, right sides out. Hold the layers together with quilt tacking (basting) spray. Quilt the layers together – you could sew simple straight lines through the centres of the bricks or either sides of the seams to hold the layers together.

3 ↓ Smooth the quilted fabric out on the floor. Measure to find the centre, and pin the piece of string to the centre of the 'quilt' and tie a marking pen to the end. You want the distance from the centre to the pen to be approximately 29" (73.7cm). Use the string/pen to draw a 58" (147.3cm) circle onto the quilt, but don't cut the circle out yet!

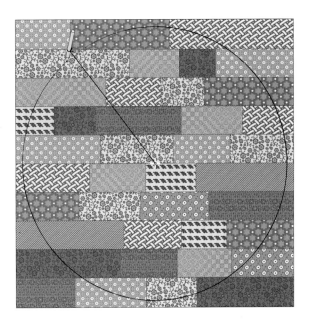

4 Make the cord tabs. Take a 2" x 42" (5 x 106.7cm) piece of purple fabric and a 2" x 42" (5 x 106.7cm) piece of navy fabric and sew them right sides together, leaving one short end open. Turn through to the right side, press and top stitch either side of the strap. Make two the same way. Cut these straps into 3½" (8.9cm) lengths to make the rope tabs. Make a total of 24. Pin these tabs around the perimeter of the circle drawn onto the quilt, raw edges of the tabs aligned with the drawn line, tabs facing inwards. Pin and tack (baste) in place. I placed 12 first at the 'hour' points (as if on a clockface) and then added tabs in between each 'hour'.

5 ↓ Sew your binding to the quilt using the double fold binding technique (see Techniques, page 31). The binding should be folded in half and the raw edges of the binding aligned with the drawn line. Use a ¼" (6mm) seam allowance. Once the binding is attached, cut along the drawn line. Turn the whole of the binding to the back of the quilt – no binding should be visible on the front of the quilt. Pin in place, then sew the binding to the back of the quilt by machine, or sew by hand, if you prefer.

7 ↓ Make the rucksack strap 'pockets' by sewing two 3½" (8.9cm) squares of navy fabric together on three sides. Turn to the right side and press, then turn under a ¼" (6mm) hem at the open edge and press. Make a total of four. Slip the ends of the shoulder straps into these pockets and then pin them to the back of the bound quilt. The top ends should be approximately 15" (38.1cm) apart and just below the binding edge. Bring the two ends at an inwards angle until they just touch and pin in place, and then sew them to the quilt by machine.

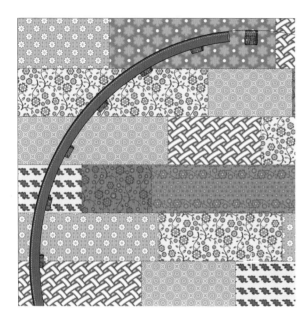

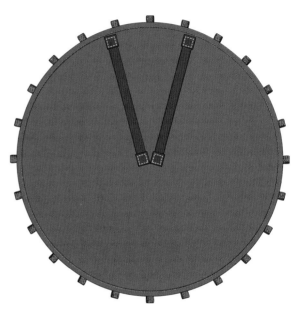

6 Make the rucksack style straps by sewing two purple 2½" x 28" (6.4 x 71cm) strips together, right sides together, leaving one short end open. Turn to the right side, press, then sew a piece of 1" (2.5cm) wide navy webbing down the centre, top stitching it in place. Make two the same.

8 Make a cord pocket in the same way, but do not attach it yet.

9 Run the cord through the loops and then knot the two ends together leaving a 7" (17.8cm) tail on each. Sew the cord pocket to the raw ends to neaten them.

```
Make it yours...

Use fabrics to match a nursery
and create a play mat and toy
bag. Decrease the size to
make versions for children to
encourage them to tidy after
they finish playing or to carry
their own things to the picnic!
```

A GREAT AFTERNOON IN

I've always loved time at home to do the things I really enjoy. The older I get, the more I value simple pleasures like a great afternoon in with my favourite craft. Whether it's crochet, knitting, English paper pieced patchwork or dressmaking, I'll happily spend a joyful afternoon or evening with my crafty bits and pieces and a few snacks.

I love to spend time crafting with friends too and the ability to make my work portable means I can drop what I'm doing at a moment's notice, grab my work and go.

From vinyl 'window' project pouches and a handy-dandy work caddy to the ultimate knit and crochet project bag and super stylish sewing machine cover, you'll find everything here for a great afternoon doing what you love best!

CRAFT CADDY AND STORAGE CUBES

I'm a crafter on the move. I split my time between crafting in my studio, at the kitchen table, or in fact any other table that finds itself empty and useful: at work, in hotel rooms, at classes. You get the picture! I take my crafting with me wherever I go and, for that, I rely on my craft caddy and storage cubes, which I have a gazillion of! Use together or apart for the most beautifully organized tools on the block.

In this project we will make folded handles, make and apply binding and use very firm fusible interfacing to create a very structured bag.

FINISHED SIZES

Craft caddy: 6" x 5" x 15" (15.2 x 12.7 x 38.1cm)
Storage cubes: 5" x 5" x 5" (12.7 x 12.7 x 12.7cm)

CRAFT CADDY CUTTING

From the outer caddy fabric and lining fabric cut:
- Base: 5½" x 15½" (14 x 39.4cm) rectangle, landscape
- Side panels: two 6½" x 15½" (16.5 x 39.4cm) rectangles, landscape
- End panels: two 6½" x 5½" (14 x 16.5cm) rectangles, portrait

Cut exactly the same pieces from fusible volume wadding (batting). Fuse the wrong side of the lining pieces to the volume wadding pieces and set aside.

Cut a base, two side panels and two end panels from the very firm fusible interfacing, ½" (13mm) smaller than listed above (so, for example, the base should be 5" x 15"/12.7 x 38.1cm). Fuse the pieces to the wrong side of the outer fabrics, centring them on the fabrics, leaving a ¼" (6mm) margin of fabric all around the edges.

→

Gather your supplies! You will need…

- Fabric

  Outer caddy and three outer storage cubes: 19¾" (0.5m)

  Outer pockets: one fat quarter

  Handles: 6" x 44" (15.2 x 112cm) strip

  Pocket bindings: 2½" (6.4cm) x WOF (width of fabric) strip

  Caddy binding: 2½" (6.4cm) x WOF (width of fabric) strip

  Handle lining: 6" x 44" (15.2 x 112cm) strip

  Lining of the caddy and three storage cubes: 19¾" (0.5m)

  Pocket lining: one fat quarter

- Very firm fusible interfacing (such as Decovil): 16" x 35½" (40.6 x 90cm)

- Firm fusible interfacing (such as Decovil Light): 16" x 35½" (40.6 x 90cm)

- Fusible volume wadding (batting) (such as Vlieseline H640): 30" x 35½" (76.2 x 90cm)

- Waist shaper: 2" x 40" (5 x 102cm)

- Threads to match your fabrics

I used quilt-weight cotton fabric throughout: a red large- and small-scale millefiori print for the outer caddy and storage cubes, the large-scale millefiori print for outer pockets and handles, and a vibrant aqua and lime green batik for caddy and cube linings, handle lining, caddy binding and pocket binding. The pocket linings won't be seen so use any cotton fabric.

From the outer pocket fabric and the pocket lining fabric cut:

- Side pockets: two 5½" x 15½" (14 x 39.4cm) rectangles, landscape
- End pockets: two 5½" (14cm) squares

Cut exactly the same pieces from fusible volume wadding (batting). Layer one outer pocket piece, one fusible volume wadding and one lining piece together, with the wadding in the centre and the fabrics on either side, right sides out. Fuse the fabrics to the wadding then use the double fold binding method (see Techniques, page 31) to bind the top edge. Use a ¼" (6mm) seam allowance. Repeat with all four pockets.

From the outer handle and handle lining fabric cut:

- Two 2½" x 20" (6.4 x 50.8cm) strips

Cut two 2" x 20" (5 x 50.8cm) strips of waist shaper, centre it on the outer pieces with a ¼" (6mm) margin on each side and fuse into place.

LET'S MAKE THE BAG!

1 ↓ Make the caddy handles. Place one outer and one lining strip right sides together. Sew along both long edges and one short side with a ¼" (6mm) seam allowance. Turn to the right side, press, and mark 4" (10.2cm) from each end. Top stitch along both sides from each either end of the strip, to the 4" (10.2cm) marks. Fold the centre 12" (30cm) section of the handle in half, lengthwise, between the 4" (10.2cm) marks, and pin. Top stitch along both edges of this centre section. Make a second handle in the same way.

2 ↓ Lay one of the handles on top of the right side of one of the outer side bag panels, 2" (5cm) down from the top edge and 3¼" (8.3cm) in from the sides, as shown. Stitch the handles in place, sewing a cross (see Techniques, page 34). Repeat with the other outer side panel and the second handle.

3 ↓ Layer the four pockets on top of the corresponding bag panels, right sides up. Align the lower edges neatly and pin, then tack (baste) the pockets in place. Divide the side pockets down the middle by top stitching down the centre. Reinforce the top of this line of stitching.

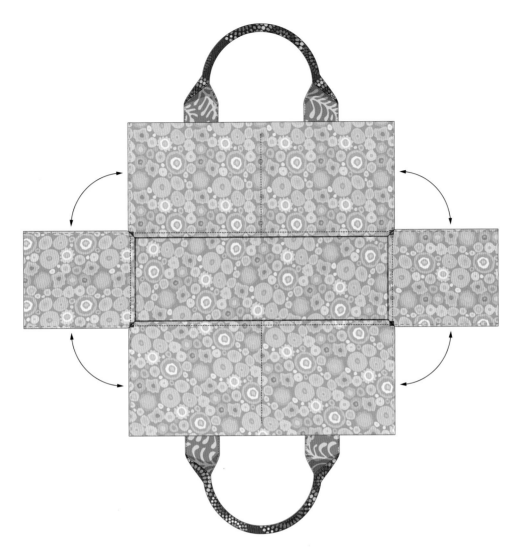

4 ↑ Assemble the outer caddy. Using the 'box bag' technique (see Techniques, page 37), sew the bag sides and ends to the base, making sure that the pockets will face the right way up. Use a ¼" (6mm) seam allowance and start and finish your seams ¼" (6mm) from the ends. Sew the sides seams in a similar way but start your seam at the very top of the caddy and finish your seam ¼" (6mm) away from the base. Turn the caddy through to the right side. Press.

5 Make the caddy lining. Sew the lining pieces together in exactly the same way as you made the outer caddy but leave it wrong side out. Drop the lining into the caddy, and align corners and all raw edges at the top. Pin, then tack (baste) in place. Use the single fold binding method (see

Techniques, page 30) to bind the top edge of the caddy with your caddy binding strip. Use a ⅜" (10mm) seam allowance to machine sew the binding to the outside of the caddy, then turn the binding to the inside and hand sew in place.

Make it yours...

Keep every measurement the same except the depth of the bag; increase to 10½" (26.7cm) (outer) and 9½" (24.1cm) (pockets) for a much deeper caddy, perfect for papercrafting, paint brushes and art supplies.

STORAGE CUBES CUTTING

Cut five 5½" (14cm) squares of outer fabric and five more of lining fabric for each cube you want to make.

Cut five squares of firm fusible interfacing, each one 5" (12.7cm).

Fuse the squares to the wrong sides of the outer fabric squares. You will need to centre them with a ¼" (6mm) margin of fabric showing all around the outer edges.

LET'S MAKE THE BAG!

1 ↓ Sew the outer squares together in a 'cross' shape with one centre square and a further four squares sewn to each edge. Lay the fabrics right sides together to join, and start and finish your seams ¼" (6mm) in from the raw edge. Use a ¼" (6mm) seam allowance. Top stitch along each seam as you go.

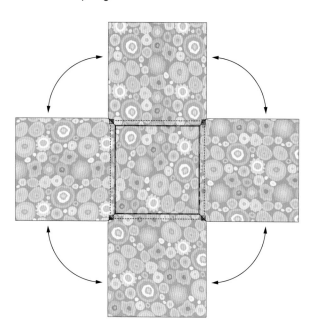

2 ↓ With right sides together, bring the outer squares up and sew the side seams to form an open topped cube. Start sewing at the very top of the seam but finish ¼" (6mm) before the bottom of the cube as before. Turn to the right side and push out the corners neatly.

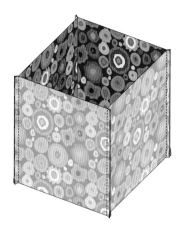

3 Repeat this process with the lining squares. Leave a 3" (7.6cm) gap in one of the base seams for turning. Leave wrong side out.

4 Insert the outer cube into the lining, right sides together, and match corner seams. Pin well. Sew around the top of the cube with a ¼" (6mm) seam allowance.

5 Turn the cube to the right side through the gap. Sew the opening closed and then pin the top edge. I rolled a tiny bit of lining to the front of the cube as I pinned to give a decorative 'binding' edge. Top stitch close to the top edge.

```
Make it yours...

You could add little handles to
the cubes — stitched on before you
sew the outer squares together.

Or make them larger and add
pockets to the inside or outside
in the same way that pockets are
added to the caddy. Interface the
pockets with a light to medium-
weight interfacing rather than
volume wadding.
```

KNIT AND CROCHET PROJECT BAG

This is the ultimate project bag for anyone who loves to knit or crochet! There's a massive space inside for your work-in-progress and it'll stay protected from light and dust with the drawstring top. The handle is detachable so you can remove it for really easy access to your work. On the outside there are a multitude of useful pockets, for up to 12 pairs of knitting needles, crochet hooks and circular needles as well as scissors and place markers. There are two huge side pockets and even bigger pockets at the front and back, great for your favourite magazine or pattern storage. You'll also find two zipped clear vinyl pockets and two poppered pockets. It's a project to take time over and is multi-skilled, but well worth the extra effort!

In this project we will make layered pockets, clear vinyl pockets, attach zips, attach poppers/snap fasteners and make a drawstring top.

FINISHED SIZES

16" x 16" x 6" (40.6 x 40.6 x 15.2cm)

CUTTING

In this project we will cut and piece different sections of the bag one at a time to keep things organized.

Gather your supplies! You will need…

- Fabric

  Outer fabric: 59" (1.5m)

  Lining fabric: 98" (2.5m)

- Sew-able clear vinyl: two 6½" (16.5cm) squares

- Fusible foam (such as Bosal In-R-Form): 34" (86cm)

- Medium-weight fusible interfacing: 6½" x 8" (16.5 x 20.3cm)

- Waist shaper or medium-weight fusible interfacing: 1½" x 32" (3.8 x 81.3cm)

- Two 1½" (3.8cm) swivel clips

- Two 1½" (3.8cm) D-rings

- 70" (180cm) Roman blind cord

- One spring loaded cord lock

- Two 7" (17.8cm) zips in a colour of your choice

- Threads to match your fabrics

- Two poppers/snap fasteners

I used a vibrant large- and small-scale millefiori cotton fabric for the outer and a mixture for the lining: 39½" (1m) of aqua and white stripe/dot fabric and 59" (1.5m) solid aqua fabric. I've used the stripe where the lining will be seen, as it's more of a contrast fabric, and then the solid has been used where it's more hidden, like lining the pockets.

LET'S MAKE THE BAG!

1 ↓ Make the crochet hook/scissor pocket. Cut a rectangle of outer fabric and lining fabric each 5½" x 3½" (14 x 8.9cm), portrait, and layer them wrong sides together. Cut a strip of lining fabric 1½" x 3½" (3.8 x 8.9cm) and use to bind the top using the single fold method (see Techniques, page 30). Make another pocket in exactly the same way using 6½" x 3½" (16.5 x 8.9cm) rectangles. Layer the shorter pocket on top of the taller one, pin/tack (baste) together, then mark lines on the shorter pocket, 1¼" (3.2cm) in from outer edges. Sew on these lines, through both pockets, to divide the smaller one. Make a total of four crochet hook/scissor pockets. Set aside.

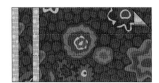

2 ↓ Make the knitting needle pocket. Cut a rectangle of outer fabric and lining fabric, each 12½" x 3½" (31.8 x 8.9cm) portrait, and layer them wrong sides together. Cut a strip of lining fabric 1½" x 3½" (3.8 x 8.9cm) and use to bind the top using the single fold method (see Techniques, page 30). Layer this pocket with a 13½" x 3½" (34.3 x 8.9cm) rectangle of outer fabric. The lower and side edges of the pocket should be aligned with the raw edges, and the top of the pocket 1" (2.5cm) down from the top. Tack in place then sub-divide the knitting needle pocket as you did the crochet pocket. Make a total of four of these knitting needle pockets.

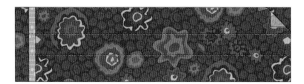

3 ↓ Now layer one of the crochet hook/scissor pockets on top of one of the knitting needle pockets, with bottom and side edges aligned. Tack the pockets together. Make a total of four of these pockets.

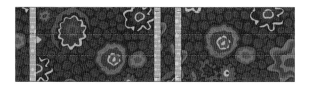

4 Make the zipped vinyl pocket. Take one of the 6½" (16.5cm) squares of clear vinyl. Cut two pieces of outer fabric 1½" x 6½" (3.8 x 16.5cm) for the top of the zip. Place one fabric strip right side up, then lay the zip right side down on top of it, with the top edge of the fabric and top edge of the zip tape aligned. Place the other rectangle of fabric on top, right side down. Sew ¼" (6mm) along the top edge to join the three pieces together, open up the fabrics and press back, then top stitch close to the zip edge.

5 ↓ To make the lower part of the zip, cut a strip of fabric 2¼" x 6½" (5.7 x 16.5cm) and turn a ¼" (6mm) in on one long edge, press. Sew the other, raw long edge to the other side of the zip, right side to right side, then turn the fabric back and fold it back on itself. The folded ¼" (6mm) edge should just meet your seam. Press, then top stitch close to the zip edge.

6 Layer the lower folded edge over the raw edge of the vinyl panel by ¼" (6mm) and top stitch it in place. The finished pocket will be 6½" (16.5cm) wide and with the addition of the zip and the fabrics your length will be a little over 8½" (21.6cm), so measure your pocket and trim a little off the bottom edge of the vinyl, if necessary.

7 Cut a piece of lining fabric 8½" x 6½" (21.6 x 16.5cm) and layer the vinyl pocket on top of this panel so that you can see the right side of the lining fabric through the vinyl window. Tack around the pocket very close to the raw edges. Make two of these lined vinyl pockets.

8 Make the pocket. Cut one rectangle of outer fabric 10 x 6½" (25.4 x 16.5cm) portrait and interface the wrong side. Fold the panel in half, wrong sides together, to create a pocket that is 6½" (16.5cm) wide and 5" (12.7cm) deep. Press, then top stitch the folded upper edge. Cut a piece of lining fabric 5½" x 6½" (14 x 16.5cm), landscape, and layer your folded pocket on top, aligning lower edges and sides. Tack in place. There should be ½" (13mm) of lining fabric showing at the top.

9 Make the flap next. Cut one piece of interfacing using the flap pattern piece (see pull-out pattern sheet). Trim the curved edges with scissors. Pin this piece of interfacing to two rectangles of outer fabric, each 4 x 6½" (10.2 x 16.5cm), right sides together. Sew around the sides and lower edge of the interfacing. Don't sew through the interfacing itself, use the edge as your sewing line. Trim the fabric to a scant ¼" (6mm), turn through to the right side and remove the pins. Press and top stitch the side and lower edges, then trim the depth to 2½" (6.4cm). On the lower edge of the flap, mark a dot ½" (13mm) up from the lower edge and 2¾" (7cm) in from the sides (this should be the centre). Attach the male part of a popper (snap fastener) at this dot. Layer the flap on top of the layered pocket, aligning the top raw edges. Mark the position of the female half of the popper on the pocket and then install the popper (see Techniques, page 39). Tack the flap in place onto the top of the pocket lining. Make a second poppered pocket in the same way. Join one

poppered pocket to the bottom of a zippered vinyl pocket using a ¼" (6mm) seam allowance. Finger press the seam and then top stitch on the vinyl. Join the second poppered pocket to the second vinyl pocket.

10 ↓ Join the knitting needle/crochet pockets to either side of the vinyl/poppered pockets using ¼" (6mm) seam allowances. Carefully open seam allowances and press flat with a wooden seam roller. Don't iron the seam or you might melt the vinyl. Cut a 2½" x 12½" (6.4 x 31.8cm) strip of lining fabric and sew to the top of the pocket panel. Make two of these panels. Set aside.

11 → Make the end pockets. Cut one rectangle of outer fabric, 13½" x 9¼" (34.3 x 23.5cm) portrait, and one strip of lining fabric 2½" x 9¼" (6.4 x 23.5cm), landscape. Sew the strip of fabric to the top of the main pocket panel. At the base of the pocket, mark the centre point and ½" (13mm) either side of the centre, make marks for the pleat. Make a second pocket in exactly the same way.

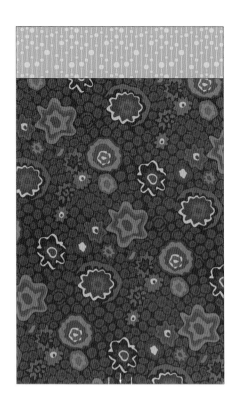

12 ↓ Arrange the side pockets and main pocket panels as shown and sew them together using a ¼" (6mm) seam allowance. Cut a lining panel 15½" x 40" (39.4 x 102cm) and lay it on top of the pocket panel, right sides together. Pin and sew along the top edge.

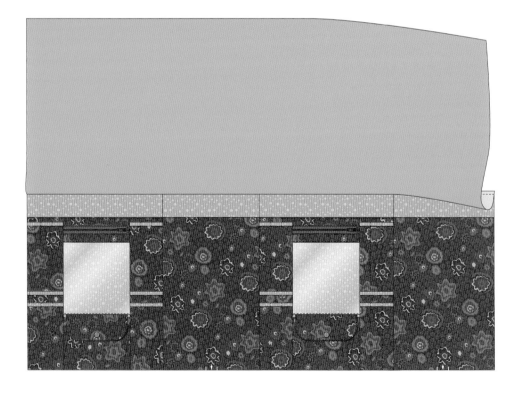

13 ↓ Open the panel out and press, then fold the panel in half, right sides together the other way, bringing the shorter sides together, lining to lining, main panel to main panel. Pin and sew this seam. Turn to the right side, fold in half so that the lining sits behind the outer panel, press and top stitch the top edge. Make the pleats at the bottom of the side pockets, bringing the outer marks into the centre, pin and tack in place.

14 Make the main bag. Cut a piece of outer fabric 16½" x 40" (42 x 102cm) landscape, and the same size piece of fusible foam. Fuse the wrong side of the fabric to the foam. Cut one base piece (see pull-out pattern sheet) from outer fabric and foam and fuse the foam to the back of the fabric.

15 ↓ Fold the main bag in half, right sides together, matching the 16½" (42cm) ends. Sew using a ¼" (6mm) seam allowance. Turn right side out.

Slide the outer pockets section onto the main bag, match lower raw edges, and pin either side of the side pocket seams. Sew from the top of the side pocket seams down to the bottom of the bag to divide the large outer pockets. This requires a little 'fabric origami'! Just bend the excess bag out of the way as you sew down the pockets. Take it slow and steady!

16 Tack around the bottom of the bag, then turn to the wrong side. Mark the quarter points – bearing in mind that the quarter points at the ends are in the centre of the side pockets and the quarter points in the front and back are in the middle of the poppered pockets. Find the quarter points on the base, then sew the base to the bag, matching the marks. Turn to the right side.

17 ↑ Make the D-ring attachments. Cut two rectangles of outer fabric and two rectangles of lining fabric each 2" x 3" (5 x 7.6cm). Pair up one outer and one lining rectangle, right sides together, and using a ¼" (6mm) seam allowance, sew both long edges. Reinforce your stitching at the start and finish off these seams to strengthen them. Turn to the right side and press. Top stitch the long edges then pass one end through a D-ring. Bring the raw ends together and tack them together very close to the raw edges. Make two, then tack the D-ring attachments either side of the bag, centring them above the side pockets.

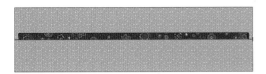

18 ↑ Make the drawstring top. Cut one strip of outer fabric 2½" x 40" (6.4 x 102cm) for the drawstring channel. Fold in half lengthways and press, then unfold and turn the short raw edges in by ¾" (19mm). Top stitch, then refold along the length. Cut two strips of lining fabric each 5½" x 40" (14 x 102cm) and layer them together, right sides touching, and sandwich the drawstring channel in between them, long raw edges aligned. Centre the channel so that there is approximately ¾" (19mm) of lining at either end. Sew along this long edge. Open out the lining pieces. you should have the channel sandwiched in between them.

19 ↑ Bring the short raw edges together and sew with a ¼" (6mm) seam allowance. Turn to the right side and fold in half, bringing the two lining pieces together, raw sides touching, and press, then top stitch very close to the channel edge. Pin the drawstring top to the bag, channel facing down, and raw edge of the drawstring top and raw edge of the bag aligned. Tack in place.

20 Make the bag lining. Cut one panel of lining fabric 16½" x 40" (42 x 102cm) and one bag base. Fold the large rectangle in half, matching the 16½" (42cm) sides. Sew this seam with a ¼" (6mm) seam allowance. Leave a 6" (15.2cm) gap in the seam for turning. Mark the quarter points on the large panel and the base and then match the points and sew the panel and base together. Insert the main bag into the lining, matching the raw edges at the top. Ensure that the D-rings are pointing down and covered by the drawstring top, which should also be pointing down. The lining should be over all of this. Sew the top of the bag with a ⅜" (10mm) seam allowance. Turn

Make it yours...

If you don't crochet you could use the lower pockets for pens, or perhaps don't divide the pocket up and have larger ones instead. The same goes for the knitting needle pockets. Undivided, these pockets would be perfect for long paint brushes or narrow quilting rulers.

the bag through the opening in the lining. Close the opening in the lining by hand or machine. Push the lining down into the bag and press the top edge neatly. With the drawstring top pushed down into the bag, top stitch around the top of the bag ¼" (6mm) in from the seam.

21 Pierce the end of the Roman blind cord with a safety pin and use this to thread the cord through the channel. Pass both ends through the spring loaded channel lock and seal the ends of the cord with a flame.

22 Make the shoulder strap. Cut a strip of outer fabric and two strips of lining fabric each 2" x 32" (5 x 81.3cm). Interface one of the lining pieces with 1½" (3.8cm) wide waist shaper or interfacing. Sew the two strips of lining fabric together with right sides facing. Sew along both long edges and one short edge, with a ¼" (6mm) seam allowance. Push through to the wrong side and press. Take your strip of outer fabric and turn ⅜" (10mm) in on both long edges. Centre this strip on top of your shoulder strap. There should be ⅛" (3mm) of the strap showing on either side. Top stitch the outer fabric strip in place down both sides. Fold 1½" (3.8cm) of the strap through a swivel clip, fold the raw edge of the strap under and stitch in place. Repeat at the other end of the strap with the second swivel clip. Attach the shoulder strap to the bag with the swivel clips.

SEWING MACHINE COVER

My sewing machine is in near constant use but I still cover it up when I'm not sewing to protect it from dust, keep things looking neat and tidy and to keep the lead, pedal, manual and extension table handy. Why stick with basic black when you can stand out from the crowd and show your true colours? Choose a vibrant or subtle print in your favourite colours and quickly sew this nifty cover.

There are two side pockets for the cables and pedal and one large pocket on the back for the manual, knee lift and extension table. The generous flap keeps everything dust-free and, when turned back, reveals essential access to your machine's carrying handle. My cover is designed to fit most large domestic sewing machines.

In this project we will make slip pockets, double fold binding and fit a twist lock.

FINISHED SIZES

20" x 13" x 9" (50.8 x 33 x 22.9cm)

CUTTING

From the main outer fabric cut:
- Front and back: two 13½" x 20½" (34.3 x 52cm) rectangles, landscape
- Sides: two 13½" x 9½" (34.3 x 24.1cm) rectangles, portrait
- Top: two 3" x 20½" (7.6 x 52cm) rectangles
- Flap: one 18" x 19" (45.7 x 48.3cm) rectangle, landscape
- Side pockets: two 9½" (24.1cm) squares
- Back pocket: one 9½" x 20½" (24.1 x 52cm) rectangle

Cut exactly the same pieces from the lining fabric.

→

Gather your supplies! You will need…

- Fabric

  Main outer fabric: 59" (1.5m)

  Pocket binding and bottom edge: 19¾" (0.5m)

  Lining: 59" (1.5m)

- Fusible foam (such as Bosal In-R-Form): 30" (76.2cm)

- Fusible volume wadding (batting) (such as Vlieseline H640): 22" (55.9cm)

- One 1¼" (35mm) twist lock

- 505 tacking (basting) spray

- Fabric marking pen

- Wonder clips

- Thread to match your fabrics

I used a really vibrant, very large-scale floral print cotton on a red and pink polka dot background for the main outer and a multi-colour stripe for the bottom edge and binding. For the lining, I used a large-scale aqua and green foliage print cotton.

From the fusible foam cut:
- Front and back: two 13½" x 20½" (34.3 x 52cm) rectangles, landscape
- Sides: two 13½" x 9½" (34.3 x 24.1cm) rectangles, portrait
- Top: two 3" x 20½" (7.6 x 52cm) rectangles

From the fusible volume wadding (batting) cut:
- Flap: one 18" x 19" (45.7 x 48.3cm) rectangle, landscape
- Side pockets: two 9½" (24.1cm) squares
- Back pocket: one 9½" (24.1cm) x 20½" (52cm) rectangle

From the binding fabric cut:
- Four 2½" (6.4cm) strips across the WOF (width of the fabric) and join them end to end with diagonal seams

LET'S MAKE THE BAG!

1 Start by making the cover top. Take the 3" x 20½" (7.6 x 34.3cm) strips of foam, outer fabric and lining fabric. Layer them together with the foam in the centre and the fabrics either side, right sides out. Fuse the fabric to the foam or use quilt tacking (basting) spray to hold the layers together. Bind one long edge using the double fold method (see Techniques, page 31). Tack (baste) around the remaining three edges ⅛" (3mm) in from the raw edges to hold the layers together. Make two pieces in the same way.

2 ↑ Make the large back pocket. Take the 9½" x 20½" (24.1 x 52cm) panels of outer and lining fabric and the fusible volume wadding (batting). Fuse the fabrics either side of the wadding, right sides out, or use quilt tacking (basting) spray. Bind

the top edge using the double fold method (see Techniques, page 31). Tack around the remaining three sides ⅛" (3mm) in from the raw edge.

3 ↓ Use this same method to make both of the side pockets.

4 Make the main structure of the cover. Take the front, back and side panels. You'll need the foam and outer fabric pieces but leave the lining pieces for now. Fuse the outer fabric panels to the foam panels and then machine or hand tack the prepared pockets in place, aligning the bottom and side raw edges.

5 Make the flap. Layer the flap outer, fusible volume wadding and lining fabrics together into a quilt sandwich, right side of fabrics on the outside, wadding in the middle. Fuse the layers together. Bind the sides and lower edge leaving the top edge unbound. Tack the top (raw) edge ⅛" (3mm) in from the edges.

6 ↗ Sew the flap to the back main panel (this is the one with the large pocket attached). Measure ¾" (19mm) in from the outer sides to centre the flap. Lay the flap down onto the panel, right sides together, raw edge of the flap 2" (5cm) down from the top. Sew along the top of the flap using a ¼" (6mm) seam allowance. Turn the flap back, covering the raw edge you just sewed, and draw a line 1" (2.5cm) from the attached edge, right across the width of the flap. Sew along this line and also top stitch along the lower edge and the sides creating a 'box' to hold the flap in place securely and to cover the raw edge.

7 Attach the cover top pieces to the front and back of the machine cover, right sides together, using a ¼" (6mm) seam allowance, starting and finishing your seams ¼" (6mm) in from the start and finish. Press back.

8 ↓ Lay out your machine cover pieces as shown. Sew the cover sides to the tops as shown. Note that the sides will extend ¼" (6mm) into the seams on the top. Start and finish these seams ¼" (6mm) in from the raw edges. Sew the side seams as shown in 'Making a box bag' (see Techniques, page 37), starting your seams ¼" (6mm) in from the corners and sewing right to the very bottom of each seam. Use ¼" (6mm) seams throughout.

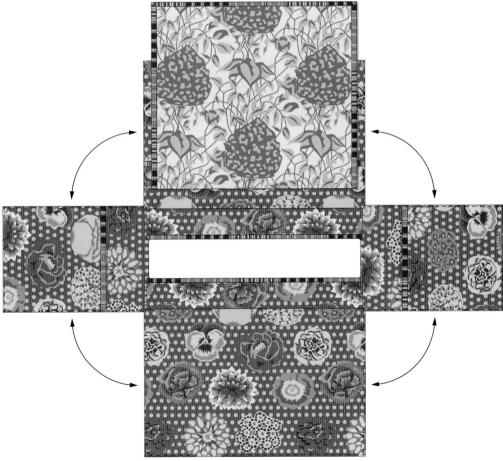

9 Turn to the right side and add the twist lock. Attach the female part to the flap, 2" (5cm) up from the lower bound edge and exactly halfway in from the sides. Pop your machine cover onto your machine and bring the flap over. Mark the required position of the male part of the twist lock through the aperture in the lock. Fix the male part of the lock into the main body of the bag. Turn back to the wrong side out again.

10 ↓ The lining is attached to the outer bag one piece at a time. Take one of the side lining pieces and lay it on the top of the bag. Align the short edge of the lining with the top of the side panel, right side of the lining touching the top of the cover. Pin or clip the edges together. Sew this seam using a ¼" (6mm) seam allowance, starting and finishing your seam ¼" (6mm) in from the ends. Add the other side piece in the same way. Flip these pieces back out of the way.

11 ↓ Add the front and back lining panels in the same way, starting and finishing seams ¼" (6mm) in from the edges. Now bring the lining pieces up and away from the main cover, and bring the side edges of the linings together. Pin and sew the side seams, starting ¼" (6mm) in from the corners and finishing at the very bottom of the seam. Turn the cover through to the right side.

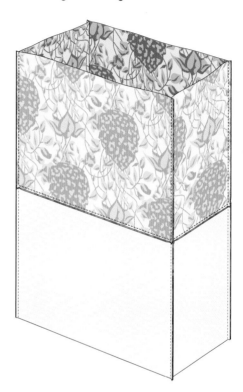

12 Bring the edges of the lining and the lower edge of the cover together and clip them together. Tack (baste) the bottom edge ⅛" (3mm) in from the raw edge. Use your remaining binding strip to bind the bottom of the cover, machine sewing to the right side and hand sewing to the inside (lining).

```
Make it yours...

The pattern is easy to resize. Measure your sewing machine as if it was a perfect
rectangle. You want the tallest and widest measurements. Now be generous! You want the
cover to slip comfortably over your machine so add 1" (2.5cm) at either end and 1"
(2.5cm) to the height. Add ½" (13mm) to all these dimensions too for your ¼" (6mm) seam
allowances. The flap is 1" (2.5cm) narrower than the main cover and doesn't need seam
allowances added to it. Remember to alter your pocket sizes too!
```

VINYL ZIPPERED PROJECT POUCH

I love to get organized for a great crafting afternoon or night in and my vinyl zippered project pouches are perfect for that, whether you're knitting socks, hand spinning yarn, crocheting granny squares, cross stitching or hand piecing patchwork... I could go on!

These pouches are such a handy size and the vinyl 'window' on each side gives great visibility while protecting your work. The bag is fully lined 'as you go' for a really neat, professional but quick result! The question is, can you stop at just one?

In this project we will sew a simple zip, make zip ends, work with vinyl, box corners and use your zig zag stitch to neaten raw edges.

FINISHED SIZES

10" x 12" x 3" (25.5 x 30 x 8cm), approx

CUTTING

From both the main outer fabric and the lining fabric cut:
- Zip: two 2½" x 13" (6.4 x 33cm) rectangles
- Base: two 4½" x 13" (11.4 x 33cm) rectangles, landscape
- Sides: four 6½" x 2¼" (16.5 x 5.7cm) rectangles, portrait

Cut the same pieces from medium-weight interfacing and fuse to the wrong side of the main outer pieces (see Techniques, page 22).

Gather your supplies! You will need…

- Fabric

  Main outer fabric: one long quarter

  Lining fabric: one fat quarter

- Sew-able clear vinyl: two 6½" x 9½" (16.5 x 24.1cm) rectangles

- One 12" (30cm) zip in a colour that tones or contrasts with your outer fabric

- Medium-weight fusible interfacing: 19¾" (0.5m)

- Threads to match your fabrics

- Wonder clips

I used a bright cotton print fabric for the outer and a bright solid in a toning colour for the lining.

LET'S MAKE THE BAG!

1   Layer the four pieces of base fabric (outer and lining) on top of each other. Measure and cut a 1½" (3.8cm) square of fabric away from the bottom two corners of all four pieces of fabric. You will need the squares in the next step. Don't touch the top corners!

2   Trim your zip to 12" (30cm). Trim a little more at the top and bottom, then take two of the 1½" (3.8cm) squares of outer fabric that you cut away in step 1. One at a time, fold ¼" (6mm) in on two opposite sides of the square and then fold in half, wrong sides together. Make two and add one to each end of the zip (see Techniques, page 25).

3   ↓ Make one of the bag fronts. Lay a 2¼" x 6½" (5.7 x 16.5cm) piece of lining fabric on the table, right side up. Lay one of the vinyl rectangles on top, aligning raw edges and then layer a 2¼" x 6½" (5.7 x 16.5cm) outer piece on top, right side down, sandwiching the vinyl between the fabrics. Use wonder clips to hold the edge together and then sew with a ¼" (6mm) seam allowance. Finger press the fabrics back away from the vinyl and make sure that the edges of both fabrics line up with each other. Top stitch very close to the sewn edge. Repeat on the other side of the vinyl rectangle.

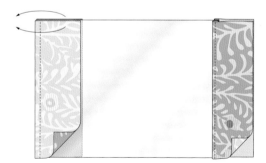

4   ↓ Now sew one of the outer and one of the lining base pieces to the bottom of the vinyl. Finger press the fabrics back and top stitch in the same way.

5   ↓ Take one of the outer zip side pieces that you cut for the top of the bag. Fold and press ¼" (6mm) along one long side. Align the other long side with the top of the bag panel, matching the strip to the fabric and vinyl. Clip in place with wonder clips. Sew with a ¼" (6mm) seam allowance, finger press back but do not top stitch yet! Now fold the top long edge (the edge you turned ¼"/6mm down on) down towards the stitched line at the back. Hold in place with clips or pin. Top stitch from the front of the bag to hold this folded edge in place.

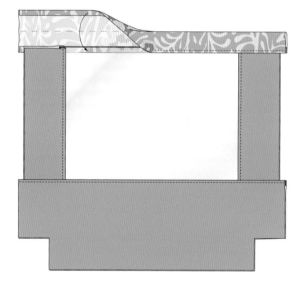

6   Make another bag panel in exactly the same way.

7   ↓ Lay out your two bag panels, with right sides up and top edges of each panel almost touching. Leave a gap of about ¼" (6mm) for the zip. Tuck the zip in place. It should be just a little shorter than the bag panels. Make sure that you leave an equal gap at both ends. Top stitch the zip in place on both sides. Open the zip fully.

8   Fold the bag in half, right sides together, matching both bag panels up. Pin together. Sew the side seams and the base seam using a ⅜" (10mm) seam allowance, then neaten your seam allowances, snipping off any loose threads and zig zag or overlock the sides and base seams.

9   Bring the side and base seams together to 'box' the bottom corners (see page 36). Pin and sew these corners, then trim threads and zig zag or overlock the corner seams. Turn the bag through to the right side and push out the corners neatly. Close the zip.

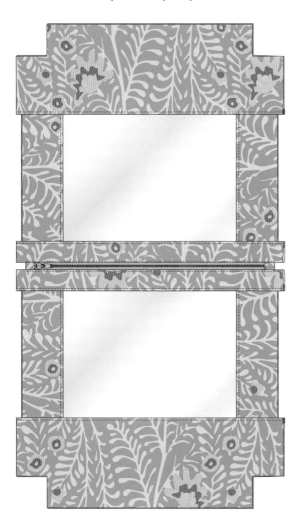

```
Make it yours...

These bags are great for all
sorts of crafts but they are
also perfect for wash bags/
toiletries. Replace the lining
fabric with waterproof fabric
and use the same fabric
to make the zip sides.
```

A MEETING IN THE CITY

Whether it's a business get-together, meeting an old friend for lunch or your daily commute to work or college, a smart and practical bag is always top of the agenda! Choose from one of three neat and stylish bags (or make them all!).

These projects include smart details like adjustable shoulder straps, zipped and flap-topped pockets and a handy key saver. My versatile messenger bag is the prefect everyday work bag while the overnight attaché is great for those last minute business trips. The city work bag even has the ability to be worn three different ways. Pick your bag and let's go to work!

ESSENTIAL MESSENGER BAG

This is, without doubt, my most popular and requested bag pattern ever! I've made this bag so many times because it's my absolute go-to for any trip into town: coffee with friends, lunch with Charlie, a quick work meeting or book signing event. There's room for all my essentials and it's a quick and easy job to transfer the contents to another bag. I've added a zippered pocket on the back of this messenger-style bag for added storage and greater security and an adjustable shoulder strap so you can wear it across your body or over your shoulder as the mood takes you!

In this project we will make a zippered pocket, an adjustable shoulder strap and sew on a magnetic bag closure.

FINISHED SIZES

10" x 9" x 3" (25.4 x 22.9 x 7.6cm)

CUTTING

From the outer main fabric cut:
- Bag front: one 10½" x 9½" (26.7 x 24.1) rectangle, portrait
- Sides: two 10½" x 3½" (26.7 x 8.9cm) rectangles, portrait
- Base: one 3½" x 9½" (8.9 x 24.1cm) rectangle, landscape

Cut the same pieces in volume wadding (batting) and fuse to the wrong side of each piece of outer fabric.

From the outer main fabric also cut:
- Back pocket lower section: one 8½" x 9½" (21.6 x 24.1cm) rectangle, landscape,
- Back pocket upper section: one 2½" x 9½" (6.4 x 24.1cm) rectangle, landscape
- Zip ends: two 1" x 5" (2.5 x 12.7cm) strips
- Shoulder strap and D-ring attachments: three 2" x 42" (5 x 106.7cm) strips

Gather your supplies! You will need…

- Fabric

  Main outer fabric: 19¾" (0.5m)

  Outer front flap: 10" (25.4cm) square of contrast fabric

  Lining fabric: 19¾" (0.5m)

- Fusible volume wadding (batting) (such as Vlieseline H640): 19¾" (0.5m)

- Firm fusible interfacing (such as Decovil Light): 19¾" (0.5m)

- Waist shaper or medium-weight fusible interfacing: 2" x 60" (5 x 152.4cm)

- One 8" (20.3cm) zip to match outer fabrics

- Two 1½" (3.8cm) rectangular rings

- One 1½" (3.8cm) rectangular strap slider

- One 4" x 1½" (10.2 x 3.8cm) faux leather magnetic satchel buckle

- Thread to match your fabrics

I used a dark charcoal grey linen-textured cotton for the main outer, and a lime jumbo polka dot cotton fabric for the lining. I used a zebra print for the outer front flap. If your design has an obvious motif you want to 'centre' or fussy cut, you might need extra.

→

From the contrast outer fabric cut:
- Bag flap: one 10" x 9½" (25.4 x 24.1cm) rectangle, portrait

Cut a piece of volume wadding to the same size and fuse to the wrong side of the bag flap (see Techniques, page 22).

From the lining fabric cut:
- Front lining: one 10½" x 9½" (26.7 x 24.1cm) rectangle, portrait
- Back and lining: two 10½" x 9½" (26.7 x 24.1cm) rectangles, portrait
- Sides: two 10½" x 3½" (26.7 x 8.9cm) rectangles, portrait
- Base: one 9½" x 3½" (24.1 x 8.9cm) rectangle, landscape
- Flap: one 10" x 9½" (25.4 x 24.1cm) rectangle, portrait
- Back pocket lower section: one 8½" x 9½" (21.6 x 24.1cm) rectangle, landscape
- Back pocket upper section: one 2½" x 9½" (6.4 x 24.1cm) rectangle, landscape

Cut firm fusible interfacing for all of the lining pieces. Cut each piece ½" (13mm) smaller than the lining pieces. Centre the pieces on the wrong side of each fabric piece and fuse into place (see Techniques, page 22).

LET'S MAKE THE BAG!

1   Start with the zippered back pocket. Make zip ends (see Techniques, page 25) for the zip and trim to 9½" (24.1cm). Sandwich the zip between the outer and lining upper sections. Sew the zip in (see Techniques, page 26) then flip the outer and lining back, press and top stitch close to the zip. Repeat with the lower outer and lining sections and the other side of the zip. Tack (baste) the zippered pocket onto the back outer panel (which is made from lining fabric don't forget!).

2   Sew the bottom half of the magnetic bag fastening to the front outer panel of your bag. Measure centre front, 1¼" (3.2cm) up from the centre front and hand stitch the closure here.

3   ↓ Sew the outer bag together. Join the front and back panels to the base first, starting and finishing your seams ¼" (6mm) in from the edges and using a ¼" (6mm) seam allowance throughout. Sew the side seams next, starting right at the top of the bag and sewing down to ¼" (6mm) before the bottom, and then finish with the bottom side seams, starting and finishing seams ¼" (6mm) in from the corners. Turn the bag to the right side and press.

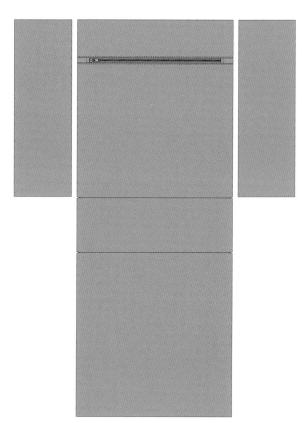

4   Make the lining for the bag in exactly the same way but this time leave a 4–5" (10–13cm) gap in one of the seams for turning. Leave the lining wrong side out.

5 ↓ Make the flap. Layer the outer and lining pieces right sides together and sew around the sides and bottom edge. Use a small round object like a jam jar lid to 'round' the corners with a pencil and then sew along these lines. Trim the excess away leaving a ¼" (6mm) seam allowance.

6 ↓ Turn the flap through to the right side and press. Top stitch the side and bottom edges. Tack the flap to the outer bag, right side of the flap against the right side of the bag back.

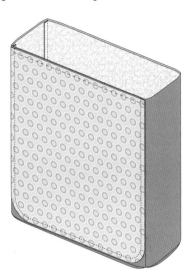

7 Make the strap and the ring attachments. Cut one of the 2" x 42" (5 x 106.7cm) strips in half and sew one full strip and one half together. Make two. Interface one of the strips with either waist shaper or fusible interfacing (see Techniques, page 22). Sew the two strips together, right sides together, sewing both long edges and one short side. Turn the strap through to the right side, press and top stitch. From this 61" (155cm) length cut two 3" (7.6cm) lengths for the ring attachments.

8 ↓ Thread a 3" (7.6cm) length of strap through a rectangular ring and bring the raw edges together. Centre this over one of the outer bag sides and tack to the upper raw edge. Repeat on the other side of the bag.

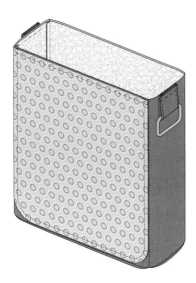

9 ↓ Place your outer bag into the lining (which should still be wrong side out), matching side seams carefully, and pin in place. Sew around the top of the bag using a ¼" (6mm) seam allowance.

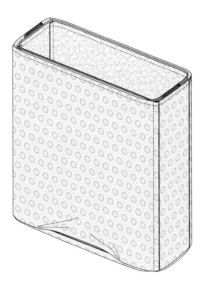

10 Turn the bag through to the right side, press and then close the gap in the lining by hand or machine. Push the lining down into the bag.

11 Pin then top stitch the top of the bag. Sew the other half of the magnetic fastening to the bag flap, making sure both halves line up perfectly.

12 Add the shoulder strap with slider (see Techniques, page 34).

Make it yours...

Use large 'sew-on' poppers (snap fasteners) to create an 'invisible' closure if you prefer. Sew these elements onto your bag in the same order as my magnetic fastener. You could always add a purely decorative button on the front of the flap if you wanted to add some extra detailing.

Add extra pockets inside your bag for further storage but don't divide them up. It's a neat and fairly narrow bag so a single pocket inside will be easier to access than two very narrow ones.

OVERNIGHT ATTACHÉ

When you need something smart and roomy, look no further than my attaché. It's the perfect size to accommodate a laptop, files, notebook and pens, but there is also space for a clean shirt or blouse and toiletries to take your day into the evening. There are two large internal pockets and two equally spacious pockets hidden under the main flap, with their own flaps to keep everything secure. I've included a key saver inside the main bag – no more rummaging in the bottom of your bag for keys!

In this project we will make a very structured bag which requires a little more experience to handle multiple stiff layers. We will use magnetic bag fasteners and make pockets with pocket flaps.

FINISHED SIZES

10" x 15" x 4" (25.4 x 38.1 x 10.2cm)

CUTTING

From the main outer fabric cut:
- Front and back: two 10½" x 15½" (26.7 x 39.4cm) rectangles, landscape
- Sides: two 10½" x 4½" (26.7 x 11.4cm) rectangles, portrait
- Base: one 4½" x 15½" (11.4 x 39.4cm) rectangle, landscape
- Front pocket: one 8½" x 15½" (21.6 x 39.4cm) rectangle, landscape

Interface these pieces with corresponding pieces of firm fusible interfacing cut ½" (13mm) smaller than the fabric pieces and centred on the fabric (see Techniques, page 22).

→

Gather your supplies! You will need…

- Fabric

  Main outer fabric: 39½" (1m)

  Feature fabric for the flaps: 19¾" (0.5m)

  Lining fabric: 39½" (1m)

- Fusible foam (such as Bosal In R Form): 19¾" (0.5m)

- Firm fusible interfacing (such as Decovil Light): 19¾" (0.5m)

- Waist shaper or medium-weight fusible interfacing: 1½" x 60" (3.8 x 152.4cm)

- Two 1½" (3.8cm) rectangular rings

- One 1½" (3.8cm) rectangular strap slider

- One ½" (13mm) swivel clip

- Two 4" x 1½" (10.2 x 3.8cm) faux leather magnetic satchel buckles

- Erasable fabric marker

- Threads to match your fabrics

I used a smart, charcoal grey linen-textured cotton fabric for the main outer, a really fun cotton print featuring palm trees and zebras for the flaps, and a zingy lime green jumbo polka dot fabric for the lining.

- Flap trim: one 3½" x 15½" (8.9 x 39.4cm) rectangle, landscape
- Shoulder strap: three 2" x 42" (5 x 106.7cm) strips (you'll line the strap with these pieces too)
- Ring attachments: four 2" x 3" (5 x 7.6cm) rectangles
- Key saver: one 2" x 8" (5 x 20.3cm) strip

From the flap feature fabric cut:
- Main flap: one 7½" x 15½" (19 x 39.4cm) rectangle, landscape
- Smaller pocket flaps: two 4½" x 7½" (11.4 x 19cm) rectangles, landscape

Make sure you centre any important designs as you are cutting these three rectangles. From firm fusible interfacing cut one 10" x 15" (25.4 x 38.1cm) rectangle to stabilize the flap but don't apply it yet.

From the lining fabric cut:
- Internal pocket: one 16" x 15½" (40.6 x 39.4cm) rectangle, portrait

Also cut a piece of firm fusible interfacing 8" x 15½" (20.3 x 39.4cm) and interface one half of the pocket piece (see Techniques, page 22).

- Front and back: two 10½" x 15½" (26.7 x 39.4cm) rectangles, landscape
- Sides: two 10½" x 4½" (26.7 x 11.4cm) rectangles, portrait
- Base: one 4½" x 15½" (11.4 x 39.4cm) rectangle, landscape
- Main flap lining: one 10½" x 15½" (26.7 x 39.4cm) rectangle, landscape

Cut these same pieces from fusible foam and fuse to the wrong side of each of the lining pieces (see Techniques, page 22).

- Small pocket flap linings: two 4½" x 7½" (11.4 x 19cm) rectangles, landscape

Interface both pieces with firm fusible interfacing cut at 4" x 7" (10.2 x 17.8cm) and centred on the back of the flaps (see Techniques, page 22).

- Front pocket lining: one 8½" x 15½" (21.6 x 39.4cm) rectangle

LET'S MAKE THE BAG!

1 ↓ Start by making the key saver. Fold the 2" x 8" (5 x 20.3cm) strip of outer fabric in half lengthwise, wrong sides together, and press. Fold the outer raw edges in to meet the centre fold and press again then fold the whole strip in half. Sew down both long edges. Thread through the small swivel clip and bring the raw ends of the strip together and tack (baste). Tack the raw ends of the key saver to the back lining piece, approximately 1½" (3.8cm) down from the top.

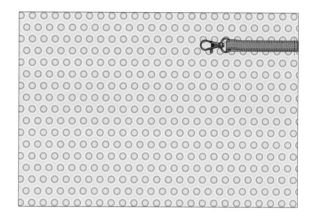

2 Make the internal pocket by folding the pocket piece in half, wrong sides together, bringing top and bottom together. Press. Top stitch very close to the top folded edge to finish and tack the sides and base together. Tack the whole pocket piece to the front lining rectangle, aligning the bottom and side edges. Mark a line up the centre of the pocket and top stitch along this line to divide the pocket into two.

3 Make the bag lining. If you haven't already done so, fuse the foam to the wrong side of each of the five main lining pieces (front, back, base and two sides). Arrange the lining pieces into a T-shape and sew together. Start by sewing the front and back lining pieces to the lining base. Use a ¼" (6mm) seam allowance, start and finish seams ¼" (6mm) in from the corners and backstitch at these points too. Leave a 5" (12.7cm) gap in one of these seams for turning the bag later. Sew the side seams in the same way, starting to sew right at the top of the bag, but finishing and back-stitching ¼" (6mm) before the base. Finally,

sew the base seams, starting and finishing ¼"
(6mm) in from the edges. See 'Making a Box Bag'
(Techniques, page 37). Set the lining aside for
now.

4   Make the outer bag flap. Sew the 3½" (8.9cm)
contrast band to the lower edge of the main flap
panel. Press the seam open and then interface
the back of the whole flap with firm fusible
interfacing. Top stitch the bag flap very close to
the seam joining the main fabric to the contrast
band. Pair the front flap with the corresponding
lining (already fused to foam), right sides
together. Sew around the sides and base seams,
use a ¼" (6mm) seam allowance and backstitch
at the start and finish. Use a small jar lid or similar
small round object to round the corners (see page
135) and trim the excess away leaving a ¼" (6mm)
seam allowance. Turn the flap through to the right
side and press. Top stitch the side and bottom
edges of the flap. Set aside.

5   ↓ Make the front (external) pockets. Pair the
interfaced outer fabric piece (8½" x 15½"/21.6 x
39.4cm) with the corresponding lining piece and
place them right sides together. Sew along the
top edge with a ¼" (6mm) seam allowance to
join them then open out and turn the lining fabric
to the back. Match the side and lower edges
carefully, press and top stitch the top edge near
to the top of the pocket. Measure 4" (10.2cm) in
from the left lower side edge of the pocket and
2" (5cm) up from the lower edge and mark a dot
with a pencil. Do the same from the right side
edge to mark the position of the lower half of your
magnetic fasteners. Centre the lower halves of
your fasteners over the pencil dots and stitch in
place by hand.

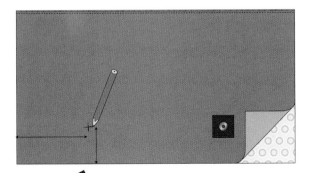

6   ↓ Place your front external pocket on top of the
outer bag front piece and match the side and
lower edges. Tack in place. Mark a line up the
centre of the pocket with an erasable pen and top
stitch to divide the pocket into two.

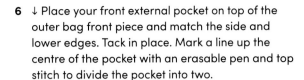

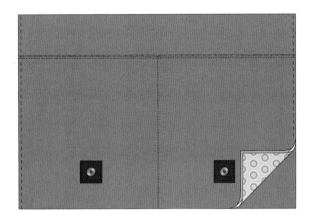

7   Make the small pocket flaps. Pair one lining and
one outer small pocket flap rectangles, right
sides together, and sew along the sides and
bottom edge with a ¼" (6mm) seam allowance.
Use a small jar lid or similar small round object
to round the lower corners as before. Sew along
these lines, then trim the corner curves leaving a
¼" (6mm) seam allowance. Turn the pocket flap
through to the right side and press. Top stitch
around the sides and lower edge. Make two.

8 ↓ Arrange the pocket flaps over the outer pockets. They will almost touch in the centre but there should be a generous ½" (13mm) gap at the outer edges. Tack the pocket flaps in place.

9 ↓ Sew the outer bag main pieces together as you did the lining, sewing the front and back to the base (no need to leave a gap this time!) and then the sides.

10 Make the ring attachments. Fuse a piece of waist shaper or interfacing to two of the four 2" x 3" (5 x 7.6cm) rectangles (see Techniques, page 22). Sew together in two pairs, one interfaced, one not, right sides together, sewing the long side edges. Turn through to the right side and press, top stitch the long edges. Thread one attachment through a rectangular ring, bring the raw edges together and tack (baste) this to the top side of the outer bag. Repeat on the other side of the bag, centring the rings and attachments.

11 Sew the flap to the outer bag. Place the flap against the back of the bag, right sides touching. Tack the flap to the top of the bag.

12 Insert the outer bag into the lining. Pin around the top of the bag, matching the side seams really carefully. Sew around the top of the bag using a ¼" (6mm) seam allowance. Turn the bag to the right side through the opening you left in the base of the lining.

13 Press the outer bag and lining, bring the raw edges of the gap in the lining together and sew by machine to close this gap. Press and top stitch the top edge of the bag to neaten and keep the lining in place.

14 Sew the upper parts of your magnetic bag fastenings to the front of the flap. Clicking the magnets of the upper and lower halves together before you start is a great way to see exactly where to place them on the flap.

15 Make the shoulder strap. Cut one of the 2" x 42" (5 x 106.7cm) strips in half (2" x 21"/ 5 x 53.3cm) and sew one half to each of the other two strips. Interface one of these 63" (160cm) lengths with a piece of waist shaper or interfacing (see Techniques, page 22). Sew the two strips together along the long edges and one short edge. Push the strap through to the right side, press and top stitch the strap, pushing in the final short edge and neatening as you do so.

16 Thread the shoulder strap through one of the rectangular ring attachments and overlap by approximately 4" (10cm). Sew a rectangular box with a cross through the middle to strengthen (see Techniques, page 34).

17 Thread the shoulder strap through the strap slider then attach the other end of the strap following general instructions for installing a strap slider (see Techniques, page 34).

```
Make it yours...

You can make the front flap
using one 10½" x 15½" (26.7 x
39.4cm) rectangle of fabric if
you prefer. This would suit a
large-scale print really well.

You could swap the magnetic
fasteners for buttons
and loops. Refer to the
instructions for making a
button loop in the pattern for
the Essential Hobo Bag (see
page 76) and make two loops.
Position them 3" (7.6cm) in
from the front flap sides and
tack in place before you make
up the flap. Once the whole
bag is put together, sew a
couple of large buttons to
the front of the bag, using
the loops to help you position
them correctly.
```

MULTI-WEAR CITY WORK BAG

My multi-wear city work bag is the perfect solution for work, college, school or going to classes. It's straightforward to make but can be carried in your hand, over your shoulder or even as a back-pack and it's super roomy with one large internal space! The large, simple rectangle front and back are the perfect place to show off fun prints, large-scale designs or even an appliquéd logo or sports badge.

In this project we will make an adjustable shoulder strap, apply a zip and make narrow straps for smaller metalware.

FINISHED SIZES

18" x 14" (45.7 x 35.5cm)

CUTTING

From the main outer fabric cut:
- Back: one 18½" x 14½" (47 x 36.8cm) rectangle, portrait
- Front top panel: one 3½" x 14½" (8.9 x 36.8cm) rectangle, landscape

Cut pieces of fusible volume wadding (batting) to the same dimensions and fuse to the wrong side of both pieces (see Techniques, page 22).

- Zip ends: two 1" x 5" (2.5 x 12.7cm) strips
- Six 2" x 42" (5 x 106.7cm) strips
- Small ring/swivel clip attachments: one 4" x 8" (10.2 x 20.3cm) strip

→

From the feature fabric cut:

• Front: one 15½" x 14½" (39.4 x 36.8cm) rectangle, portrait

If your fabric has a design you want to highlight, make sure you centre this before you cut the fabric panel out. Cut a piece of volume wadding (batting) to the same size and fuse to the wrong side of the panel (see Techniques, page 22).

From the lining fabric cut:

• Back: one 18½" x 14½" (47 x 36.8cm) rectangle, portrait
• Lower bag front: one 15½" x 14½" (39.4 x 36.8cm) rectangle, portrait
• Upper bag front: one 3½" x 14½" (8.9 x 36.8cm) rectangle, landscape

LET'S MAKE THE BAG!

1 Start by making the wide straps. Sew three 42" (106.7cm) lengths together to make 126" (3.2m). Make two like this. Interface one of the lengths with waist shaper or medium-weight interfacing (see Techniques, page 22). Pair the strips together, right sides facing, and sew both long edges and one short edge. Turn through to the right side and press. Top stitch the long edges. From this length cut two pieces, each 50" (127cm), for the long straps. To one of the straps, add a swivel clip at one end and a strap slider and a swivel clip at the other end. To the other strap, add a swivel clip to one end and a strap slider and D-ring to the other (see Techniques, page 34). Set aside.

2 From the remainder cut one 9" (22.9cm) strip for the top handle, two 5" (12.7cm) pieces for the side ring attachments and two 3" (7.6cm) pieces for the bottom ring attachments. You should have 1" (2.5cm) left which you can discard.

3 Make the small strap next. Fold the 4" x 8" (10.2 x 20.3cm) rectangle in half lengthways, wrong sides together. Press, then open out and turn the long raw edges in to meet the centre crease. Press again, then fold the whole strip in half one more time along the centre fold to create a 1" (2.5cm) wide neatened strip. Top stitch both long edges. Cut two 3½" (8.9cm) lengths from this and discard the remaining 1" (2.5cm). Thread one piece through the small swivel clip and bring the raw edges together. Tack (baste). Do the same with the other piece and the small D-ring. Again tack the raw ends together.

```
Make it yours...

Use a super-chunky zip and decorative
zip pull to really draw attention!

Decorate or appliqué the lower part
of your bag. Use college football
badges, decorative patches or braid
to customize your bag.
```

4 Layer the outer back panel with the interfaced lining piece, wrong sides together (right sides of both fabrics on the outside). Tack (baste) the panels together by sewing very close to the edges or use quilt tacking (basting) spray.

5 ↓ Make the front of the bag. Shorten your zip to 13" (33cm) and then add the zip ends (see Techniques, page 25). Trim the neatened zip to 14½" (36.8cm). Sandwich the zip between the outer upper rectangle and the lining upper rectangle. Sew the zip in place, then flip the outer and lining away from the zip, press and top stitch close to the zip. Repeat with the lower outer and lower lining. Tack all around the outer edge very close to the raw edges.

6 ↓ Mark the centre at the top of the front panel. On the main fabric, tack the 9" (22.9cm) handle 1½" (3.8cm) either side of the centre mark then tack the small straps with their corresponding swivel clip and D-ring to the top centre directly on top of the short handle. Slip a 5" (12.7cm) length of wide strap through a large swivel clip and tack 1" (2.5cm) down from the top left side corner. Angle the strap at 45 degrees inwards, as shown. Do the same on the right side but use a D-ring this time. Slip a 3" (7.6cm) length of wide strap through a large D-ring, bring the raw edges together and tack to the bottom edge, 2" (5cm) in from the corner. Repeat on the other bottom corner, 2" (5cm) in, using the last large D-ring.

7 Layer the front of the bag on top of the back, right sides together, making sure that all straps and metalware are facing inwards and the zip is partially opened. Sew around the outside of the bag using a ¼" (6mm) seam allowance. Neaten the seam allowance with a wide zig zag stitch and trim any loose threads. Turn your bag to the right side and press. Attach the shoulder straps and you're good to go!

A WEEKEND IN THE COUNTRY

Whether it's a grand country house hotel, a village pub or staying with friends, there really is nothing like a few days in the country to clear the cobwebs and revitalize the soul. Even a work trip can be turned into an adventure – I always try to explore the local area whenever I travel.

Packing for a few days away can be made simple with my trio of weekend bags. My roll-up bathroom organizer contains all the pockets you need for mini toiletries, hair care, dental products and scent and can be hung on a hook for easy access. My essential toiletry bag combines the storage potential of a zippered bag with added functionality in the form of a flap filled with pockets. My weekend warrior bag is a pretty simple make, but provides plenty of room for a few days away and there are pockets inside and out to make sure you arrive organized and ready to enjoy your break.

THE WEEKEND WARRIOR

A weekend in the country requires a fabulous bag with enough space for plenty of outfit changes, activewear and maybe a bottle of champagne too! My weekend warrior bag ticks all the boxes and does so in style. There's loads of room inside and I've kept the interior simple to allow for maximum packing space. On the outside, there are large pockets at either end, handles for carrying the bag at your side or over one shoulder and I've also included a detachable and fully adjustable shoulder strap. The front and back panels are simple and uncluttered, allowing you to use large-scale and feature prints without the distraction of zips or pockets.

In this project we will use a 'luggage style' double zip, add zip tabs, which make opening and closing a bag so much easier, make pockets with faux binding, sew simple curves and make fixed and detachable/adjustable shoulder straps.

FINISHED SIZES

12" x 16" x 10" (30 x 40.6 x 25.4cm)

CUTTING

From fabric A cut:
- Front and back panels: two 21" x 14½" (53.3 x 36.8cm) rectangles, portrait, centring any important elements of the design
- End pockets: two 9½" x 10½" (24.1 x 26.7cm) rectangles, landscape

From fabric B cut:
- Four bag ends (two for the outer bag and two for the lining) using the pull-out pattern sheet
- Main lining panels: two 21" x 16½" (53.3 x 42cm) rectangles, portrait

→

Gather your supplies! You will need…

- Fabric

  Outer fabric A for the bag front, back and outer pocket fronts: 39½" (1m)

  Outer fabric B for the bag ends: 39½" (1m)

  Outer contrast fabric C for the front and back edges, fixed handles, shoulder strap, zip pulls and pocket linings/faux binding: 29½" (0.75m)

- Medium-weight fusible interfacing: 39½" (1m)

- Fusible foam (such as Bosal In-R-Form): 39½" (1m)

- One 18" (45.7cm) length of continuous zip plus two zip pulls

- Two 1½" (3.8cm) D-rings

- Two 1½" (3.8cm) swivel clips

- One 1½" (3.8cm) strap slider

- Wonder clips

- Threads to match your fabrics

For outer fabric A (bag front, back and outer pockets), I used a large-scale yellow 'Chinese dragon' print, which also had a peony flower design on it that I used for the pockets. The design was so large I used 78¾" (2m) of fabric but there was lots left over – it didn't go to waste of course – I made the toiletry bag and bathroom roll-up with the leftovers! For outer fabric B and the lining I used a blue and white 'tile' print. For the contrast fabric C, I used a vibrant pink/red floral.

From fabric C cut:

- End pocket linings: two 10 x 10½" (25.4 x 26.7cm) rectangles, landscape
- Strap and D-ring pockets: six 2½" x 3½" (6.4 x 8.9cm) rectangles
- Seven 2" (5cm) strips each WOF (width of fabric)
- Main panel contrast edges: four 1½" x 21" (3.8 x 53.3cm) strips
- Zip pulls: two 1½" x 5" (3.8 x 12.7cm) strips

From medium-weight interfacing cut:

- End pockets: two 10" x 10½" (25.4 x 26.7cm) rectangles
- Shoulder strap and handles: 1½" x 140" (3.8cm x 3.6m) total length (we will also cut D-ring attachments from this strap)

From fusible foam cut:

- Two bag ends, using the pull-out pattern sheet
- Main bag panels: two 16½" x 21" (42 x 53.3cm) rectangles

```
Make it yours...

I've used a really bold
feature fabric to make a
statement, but this bag would
look fabulous in a solid or a
smaller design.

The contrast strips at either
side frame the main bag panels
beautifully, but you can leave
them off. Just cut the main
front and back panels the same
size as the linings: 21" x
16½" (53.3 x 42cm).

Substitute 1½" (3.8cm) wide
webbing for the carry handles
and shoulder strap for a
faster finish.

Add zippered pockets inside
your bag using the 'letterbox'
zip pocket method or add
simple patch pockets if you
prefer (see Techniques, pages
28 and 23-24).
```

LET'S MAKE THE BAG!

1 Make the shoulder strap, handles, D-ring attachments, zip tabs and zip pulls. Use three of your WOF x 2" (5cm) strips of fabric. Cut one in half and then join one half to each of the other two 40" (102cm) strips to create two 2" x 60" (5 x 152.4cm) strips. Fuse interfacing centrally to the wrong side of one of them, place the two strips right sides together and sew along one short and both long sides with a ¼" (6mm) seam allowance. Turn the shoulder strap through to the right side, fold in the raw short end to neaten and then press and top stitch. Thread one end through a swivel clip and fold back around 2" (5cm) of strap to overlap. Sew in place in a box with a cross through the middle (see Techniques, page 34). Thread the other end through the strap slider, then through the remaining swivel clip and then pass the end of the strap back under the buckle bar of the slider. Finally position the end of the strap back on itself, lining to lining, and sew in place in a box with a cross through the middle (see Techniques, page 34). Set aside.

2 For the carry handles, fuse interfacing centrally to the wrong side of another WOF x 2" (5cm) strip, place a second strip right sides together and sew along one short and both long sides with a ¼" (6mm) seam allowance. Turn the handle through to the right side. Fold in the raw short end to neaten and then press and top stitch. Repeat to make a second handle. Trim two 3" (7.6cm) lengths from one of the handles and use these short lengths for the D-ring attachments. Fold one through a D-ring and bring the raw edges together. Machine tack (baste) the edges together very close to the edge. Make two. The remaining handle should be 34" (86.4cm). Set this to one side.

3 Trim two 2½" (6.4cm) lengths from the **other** handle to use for the zip tabs. Fold them in half and tack the raw edges together (see Techniques, page 25). Make two. And then trim 1" (2.5cm) from the handle and discard, leaving a second 34" (86.4cm) handle. Place a pin 5" (12.7cm) in from both ends of one handle, fold the centre 24" (61cm) of the handle in half and hold with wonder clips. Sew close to the edge of this centre 24" (61cm) length. Make two and set aside.

4   Finally make the zip pulls. Take one 1½" x 5" (3.8 x 12.7cm) strip of fabric C and fold in half lengthwise, unfold and then fold the raw edges into the middle crease, turn the ends in about ¼" (6mm) and press. Finally, fold the whole strip back in half down the original centre line, right sides out. Top stitch down either side of this narrow strip. Make two.

5   Make the D-ring and handle pockets. Take one 2½" x 3½" (6.4 x 8.9cm) rectangle. Fold and press a ¼" (6mm) allowance towards the wrong side of both of the short ends. Fold the rectangle in half, right sides together, and sew the short (unfolded sides) with a ¼" (6mm) seam allowance. Turn through to the right side and press. Make a total of six. Set aside for the time being.

6   ← Make the outer side panels. Fuse a fabric B outer to a corresponding piece of fusible foam. Make the pocket by first interfacing the wrong side of the outer pocket piece (see Techniques, page 22), then sewing the top edge of the pocket outer to the top edge of a pocket lining, right sides together, with a ¼" (6mm) seam allowance. Flip the lining to the back of the pocket and match bottom and side edges. Press. This will create a ¼" (6mm) faux binding on the right side of the pocket front. Top stitch close to the edge of the faux binding.

7 ↓ Layer the pocket on top of the side panel, matching side and bottom edges. Tack in place. Slip one prepared D-ring into one of the little pockets made in step 5. Position this pocket ¼" (6mm) above the outer pocket and centred. Sew the pocket in place in a square with a cross through the middle for strength (see Techniques, page 34). Make the two bag ends in the same way.

8 ↓ Make the bag front and back. Sew the 1½" x 21" (3.8 x 53.3cm) strips of fabric C to either side of the main bag front panel, use a ¼" (6mm) seam allowance and press the seams towards the contrast edges. Fuse the panel to the corresponding piece of foam. Slip the raw ends of a pre-prepared handle into two more of the little pockets made in step 5 and position the top edge of each little pocket 8" (20.3cm) down from the top of the main bag panel and 2½" (6.4cm) in from the sides. Sew the handles in place using a square and cross (see Techniques, page 34). Make a bag back in exactly the same way.

9 ← Add the zip. Fit both metal zip pulls onto the zip tape making sure that the rounded 'front' of the zip pulls meet in the middle. Position the wrong side of the zip on top of one of the main bag panels. Sew the zip to the panel using a zipper foot, then turn the zip to the right side. Push the seam allowance away towards the main bag panel and press, then top stitch near to the edge. Sew the other side of the zip tape to the other main bag panel. Finally, tack the pre-prepared zip tabs at either end of the zip, with the loops pointing inwards, as shown, and the raw ends aligned.

10 ↓ With right sides facing, bring the lower edges of the bag together and sew the bottom seam. I used a slightly bigger seam allowance here, ⅝" (1.6cm), and I stitched it twice for added strength. Press this seam open. Pin or wonder clip one bag end into place. Match the centre top of the bag end with the middle of the zip and pop a wonder clip in place to hold. Repeat with the centre bottom of the bag end and the bottom seam of the main bag. Bring the edges of the main bag and the bag end together and clip in place. Sew the seam (back to using a ¼" (6mm) seam allowance here). Add the other end in the same way – make sure before you do this that the zip is at least partially open! Press seams towards the main bag. Keep the bag wrong side out.

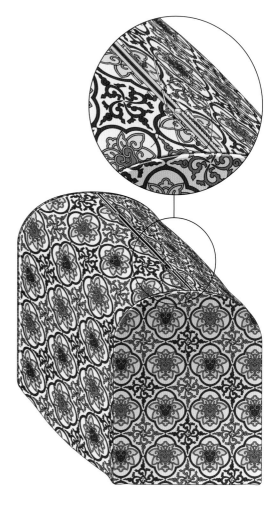

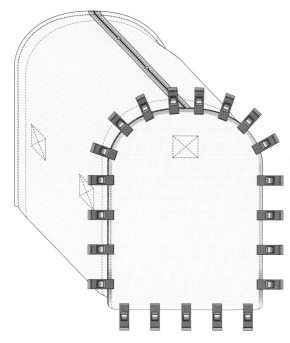

11 Make the lining. Take one main lining panel and fold the top long edge in towards the wrong side by ¼" (6mm). Press, then repeat with the other main lining panel. Sew the two panels together along the bottom long raw edges. Use a ⅝" (1.6cm) seam allowance again. Press the seam open. Pin the side edges of the main lining panel to the ends as before. This time there's no zip! You'll need to leave about ½" (13mm) gap between the two neatened edges at the top to leave room for the zip. Sew the side panels on using a ¼" (6mm) seam allowance.

12 ↑ Turn the lining to the right side and press. Insert the bag into the lining and match up the sides neatly. The neatened edges down the centre of the bag should be pinned either side of the zip. The edges of the lining should just come up to your stitching on the zip. Hand sew the lining to the zip edges taking care to make tiny stitches that will not show from the right side.

13 Turn the bag to the right side and press lightly, if necessary. Thread a pre-prepared fabric zip pull through the metal zip pull and tie tightly. Do the same with the other zip pull. Attach the shoulder strap to the D-rings using the swivel clips or pop the strap in one of the side pockets for later use.

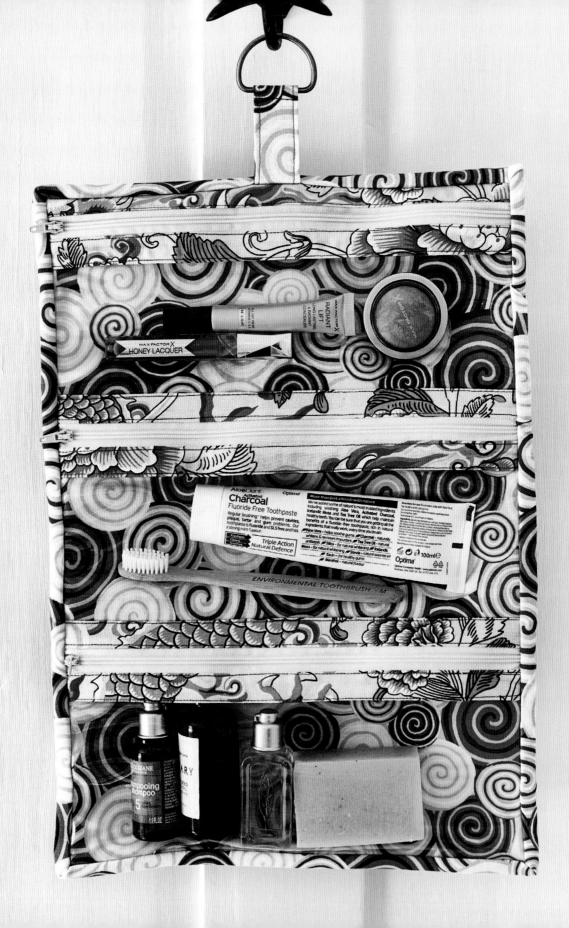

ABSOLUTE ESSENTIALS ROLL-UP BATHROOM ORGANIZER

An overnight stay with friends or in a hotel can feel like a lot to organize, but my absolute essentials roll-up bathroom organizer takes care of your toiletries and provides safe passage and a hanging tidy for when you arrive. Simply unroll, hang up on a hook and you're 'unpacked' and ready to go!

In this project we will sew in zips with bound edges, use clear vinyl to make pockets, make ties and add a double fold binding to the edge of the project.

FINISHED SIZES

Unrolled: 16" x 11" (40.6 x 28cm)

CUTTING

From the main outer fabric cut:
- One 16½" x 11½" (42 x 29.2cm) panel, portrait
- Six 2" x 13" (5 x 33cm) strips, landscape

From the inner lining fabric cut:
- One 16½" x 11½" (42 x 29.2cm) panel, portrait
- Enough 2½" (6.4cm) wide strips to make a 60" (152.4cm) length when sewn together
- Ring tab: one 4" x 5" (10.2 x 12.7cm) strip
- Ties: two 2" x 14" (5 x 35.5cm) strips

From the clear vinyl cut:
- Three 4½" x 11½" (11.4 x 29.2cm) rectangles

Gather your supplies! You will need…

- Fabric

  Main outer and zip edges: 19¾" (0.5m)

  Inner lining, binding, ring tab and ties: 19¾" (0.5m)

- Sew-able clear vinyl: 19¾" (0.5m)

- Three 12" (30cm) zips

- One 1½" (3.8cm) D-ring

- Quilt-weight wadding (batting): 11½" x 16½" (29.2 x 42cm)

- 505 quilt tacking (basting) spray

- Wonder clips

- Thread to match your fabrics

I've used a bright yellow Chinese-style floral for the main outer flap, and a blue and white geometric 'tile' print for the inner lining bag.

LET'S MAKE THE BAG!

1 Lay your 16½" x 11½" (42 x 29.2cm) panel of outer fabric wrong side up on your work surface and cover with the piece of quilt wadding (batting). Lay the matching piece of inner fabric on top, right side up, and use quilt tacking (basting) spray to hold the three layers together.

2 Prepare the zip bindings. Take one of the 2" x 13" (5 x 33cm) strips of outer fabric and turn in ¼" (6mm) along one long edge towards the wrong side. Press. Align the unturned long edge of the strip with one side of the zip, right sides touching and raw edges aligned. Use a zipper foot and sew along the fabric to join it to the zip. Press the fabric away from the zip, then turn the other long edge (the one with the turned edge) to the wrong side of the zip. Cover the line of stitching with the folded edge of the strip, pin in place, then top stitch from the front, very close to the edge of the fabric, top stitching and catching the back edge of the binding at the same time. Repeat on the other side of the zip. Prepare all three zips in this way (see Techniques, page 27).

3 ↓ On the wrong side of the lower edge of each zip binding mark a ¼" (6mm) line with a pencil. Align the edge of your vinyl 4½" x 11½" (11.4 x 29.2cm) panel with this line and from the wrong side, sew very close to the bottom edge of the fabric binding to join the zip to the vinyl. Do this with all three zips and the three vinyl pieces.

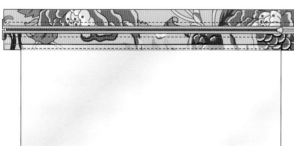

4 ↓ Align your first vinyl pocket with the lower edge of your main panel, layering the pocket on top of the lining side, so the zip is right side up. Use wonder clips to hold in place, then tack the pocket in place ensuring that the zip pull is within the main panel and your tacking stitches. Tack the pocket on the lower and side edges only and leave ½" (13mm) un-tacked at the top side edges.

5 Align your next pocket above the first, tucking a generous ¼" (6mm) of vinyl underneath the fabric zip binding of the lower pocket. Hold in place with clips. Tack (baste) the sides, leave ½" (13mm) un-tacked at the top of the pocket sides, as before, then top stitch across the bottom of the pocket, just into the bottom pocket fabric binding. This line of top stitching creates the bottom of the second pocket and finishes the top edge of the lower pocket in one step!

6 ↓ Add the third pocket at the top of the panel. Leave ¾" (19mm) gap at the very top and then position the last pocket, tucking the lower edge of the vinyl under the second pocket. Tack the sides completely this time, then top stitch the top of the last pocket and the lower edge.

7 ↓ Make the ring tab. Fold the long edges of the 4" x 5" (10.2 x 12.7cm) strip of fabric in to meet the centre, wrong sides together, then fold the strip in half and press. Top stitch both long edges. Thread this tab through the D-ring and bring the raw edges together. Tack together. Centre the raw edges of the tab over the top centre of your main panel, on the lining side and with the D-ring hanging down. Tack in place.

8 ↓ Make the ties. Take one of the 2" x 14" (5 x 35.6cm) tie pieces and fold and top stitch just as you did for the D-ring tab in step 7, but also fold in one short end neatly and stitch that too. Make two of these ties. Position the ties at the same point as the D-ring, but on the outside this time. Tack in place.

9 If you haven't done so already, sew the binding strips together to create a 60" (152.4cm) piece. A diagonal seam is less bulky. Press your binding strip in half, wrong sides together. Cut one end at a 45° angle, turn and press a ½" (13mm) hem to neaten it. Starting with the neatened edge of the binding and working on the inside (pocket side) of the panel, bind the panel following the instructions for double fold binding (see Techniques, page 31).

10 Turn the binding to the outside of the panel and hand-sew the binding in place.

Make it yours...

Divide the pockets vertically by stitching through the vinyl and the lower part of each zip binding. Don't stitch over the teeth! Stop stitching about ¼" (6mm) before you get to the zip teeth.

This hanging organiser would be really useful for artists' materials, make-up brushes, papercrafting tools and ink pads, cake decorating tools and toppings – you get the idea. It's very versatile!

ESSENTIAL TOILETRY BAG

Zippered pouches are super-useful for all kinds of applications, but I've taken this simple bag to the next level with a multi-function flap! The flap creates a sleeve to tuck a face cloth or small towel into – fantastic for taking on long flights for a rejuvenating freshen up. The flap includes a covered pocket for make-up brushes and a clear vinyl zippered pocket for other small essentials like lip balms, make-up or hand sanitizer.

In this project we will make a vinyl zipped pocket, make ties, put in a basic zip and 'box' corners.

FINISHED SIZES

8" x 10" x 2" (20.3 x 25.4 x 5cm)
Flap extension: 13" x 8" (33 x 20.3cm)

CUTTING

In this project we will cut and piece different sections of the bag one at a time to keep things organized.

LET'S MAKE THE BAG!

1 Cut the pieces for the main bag. From both the outer fabric and inner lining fabric, cut two 8½" x 11½" (21.6 x 29.2cm) rectangles, landscape. From the firm fusible interfacing and the firm wadding (batting) cut two 11" x 8" (28 x 20.3cm) rectangles. At the bottom two corners of each rectangle mark and cut away a 1" (2.5cm) square for boxing the base corners later. Fuse the firm interfacing to the outer fabric rectangles, and the fleece to the lining rectangles, positioning the interfacing or wadding an even ¼" (6mm) in from all sides of the fabric (see Techniques, page 22). Also from the lining fabric, cut four 1" x 1½" (2.5 x 3.8cm) rectangles for the zip ends, a 1" x 5" (2.5 x 12.7cm) strip for the swivel clip tab and a 2" x 5" (5 x 12.7cm) strip for the D-ring tab.

2 ↓ Take the 2" x 5" (5 x 12.7cm) strip of fabric and fold a scant ¼" (6mm) in on both long edges, wrong sides together, press, then fold your strip in half and press. Top stitch along both long edges to create the D-ring tab. Thread the tab through the D-ring and bring the raw ends together. The tab is a bit too long at this stage (but it's easier to make and top stitch a longer tab!) so trim the folded tab to 1½" (3.8cm) and then tack it to the centre bottom of one of the main outer fabric/interfacing rectangles.

3 ↓ Mark a 9½" (24.1cm) section of the 12" (30cm) zip. Add zip ends to the zip at this point by sandwiching the zip end between two 1" (2.5cm) x 1½" (3.8cm) strips of lining fabric, right sides of the fabric touching either side of the zip. Sew across the zip with a ¼" (6mm) seam allowance, flip the zip ends back and press, then top stitch close to the seam. Repeat at both ends of the zip. Measure your zip from one zip end to the other, ensuring that you have at least 11½" (29.2cm) of zip. Trim the excess zip from each end.

4 ↓ Sandwich the prepared zip, right side down, onto the top edge, right side of one of the outer bag rectangles, matching ends. Pin and tack in place. Now place the corresponding lining piece on the wrong side of the zip, top edge aligned and the right side of the outer bag touching the right side of the lining. Sew the zip in place using a zipper foot. Press the lining and outer bag away from each other, bring the lower edges together and press flat, then top stitch close to the edge of the zip. Repeat with the other bag outer and lining section. Set aside.

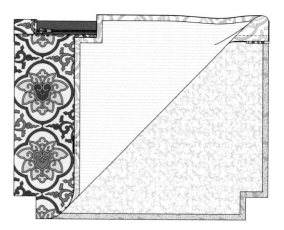

5 ↓ Make the flap. From both the outer and lining fabrics, cut one 14½" x 8½" (36.8 x 21.6cm) rectangle, portrait, and from both firm fusible interfacing and wadding (batting), cut a 8" x 14" (20.3 x 35.5cm) rectangle. At the bottom (short) edge of each piece, use an egg cup or small saucer to round off the corners very slightly. Mark the curve and trim the excess fabric away. Fuse the interfacing to the outer fabric and the fleece to the lining, positioning the interfacing/wadding ¼" (6mm) inside the fabric on all sides (see Techniques, page 22). Take the 1" x 5" (2.5 x 12.7cm) strip of lining fabric that you cut earlier and fold a scant ¼" (6mm) in on both long edges, wrong sides together. Fold, then press the strip in half to create a narrow 5" (12.7cm) long neatened strip. Top stitch along both long ends. Pass the tab through your swivel clip, bringing the raw ends together. Position the swivel clip on the right side, centre of your main flap outer fabric. You want the bottom edge of the swivel clip ½" (13mm) in from the raw edge of your flap. Tack in place.

6 ↓ Make the pockets for the flap. From the outer fabric, cut two 5½" x 6½" (14 x 16.5cm) rectangles, landscape, for the brush pocket and flap. Also cut one 5½" x 6½" (14 x 16.5cm) rectangle from the lining fabric for the pocket flap lining and one 6" x 6½" (15.2 x 16.5cm) rectangle for the pocket lining. Finally, cut one 5" x 6" (12.7 x 15.2cm) rectangle of firm fusible interfacing for the pocket flap. Pair one outer fabric rectangle and the 6" x 6½" (15.2 x 16.5cm) rectangle of lining fabric, right sides together. Sew across the top 6½" (16.5cm) edge with a ¼" (6mm) seam allowance. Open out the fabrics and press the seam allowance towards the lining fabric. Flip the lining fabric to the back of the pocket and align the lower raw edges. This will leave about ¼" (6mm) of the lining fabric showing on the front of the pocket. Press and then top stitch close to the faux binding edge on the pocket. Fold the side edges in by ¼" (6mm) and press.

7 ↓ Position the pocket 1¾" (4.4cm) up from the bottom edge of the main flap lining. Top stitch the sides of the pocket onto the flap lining and Tack (baste) the bottom raw edge. Divide the pocket by top stitching vertical lines at 1" (2.5cm) to 1½" (3.8cm) intervals through the pocket and flap.

8 ↓ Make the pocket flap. Use the same egg cup or small saucer you used to round the corners of the main flap to round the corners of the pocket flap, lining and interfacing. Fuse the interfacing to the outer fabric, ¼" (6mm) in from the fabric edges. Place the outer and lining fabrics right sides together and sew around the sides and curved base. Leave the top edge open. Turn to the right side and press. Top stitch on the three sewn sides. Tack the pocket flap onto the main flap lining piece, aligning the raw edge of the pocket flap with the raw edge of the main flap.

9 ↓ Make the clear vinyl zippered pocket. From the outer fabric cut two 2" x 12" (5 x 30cm) strips and turn under a ¼" (6mm) allowance along one long edge of each strip. Press. Take one strip of outer fabric and lay it on top of your zip, right sides facing and top edge of fabric aligned with top edge of zip. Sew close to the edge of the zip using a zipper foot. Turn the fabric back and press, then fold the fabric to the wrong side of the zip and align the prefolded edge with the line of stitching and cover it. Top stitch very close to the prefolded edge of the fabric. Repeat on the other side of the zip with the second strip of fabric.

10 Cut a 3" x 8½" (7.6 x 21.6cm) piece of clear vinyl and position the bottom edge of the zip you have just prepared over the top raw edge of the vinyl, overlapping by ¼" (6mm). Carefully top stitch the zip in place. Cut a strip of fabric 1¼" x 10" (3.2 x 25.4cm), turn and press a ¼" (6mm) hem along both long edges. Top stitch one of these edges to the lower edge of your vinyl pocket and then position this pocket on the flap lining, 1½" (3.8cm) away from the brush pocket. Top stitch along the bottom edge of the fabric trim to attach the lower edge of the pocket and then sew along the top edge of the zip trim to attach the top edge of the pocket. Tack the sides of the pocket to the flap and then trim excess zip from the sides.

11 ↓ Layer the flap outer fabric/interfacing piece over the flap lining, right side of the outer touching the right side of the pocket. Pin, then sew along the sides and curved edge, leaving the straight short side open. Turn to the right side and press. Top stitch around the flap, being sure to fold the flap of the brush pocket in. The swivel clip should be pulled up away from the flap. Also add quilt lines ¼" (6mm) apart in the first 1¾" (4.4cm) of the flap and in the middle gap between the brush pocket and the clear vinyl pocket. This quilting will help the flap to bend at the appropriate points.

12 ↓ Position the flap on the lower edge of the main bag piece, main outer fabrics touching. Fold the lining of the main bag out of the way and tack the flap in place.

Make it yours...

If you don't want a vinyl pocket, replace it with one cut from lining fabric.

Divide the brush pocket at wider or narrower increments to suit your needs. You could just divide the pocket in two to provide a home for toothbrush and toothpaste.

Use the same principles of adding pockets to the inside of a bag flap — try using with the Essential Messenger Bag pattern (see page 132).

13 ↓ Open the main bag pieces away from the lining pieces and align lining with lining and outer with outer. Pin the pieces together, making sure the flap is tucked inside out of the way. Sew the side and end seams with a ¼" (6mm) seam allowance, leaving the cut-out corners unstitched to make box corners later. Leave a 4" (10.2cm) gap in the bottom of the lining for turning.

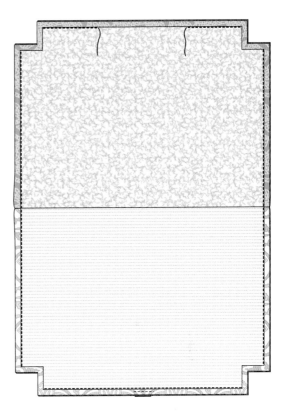

114 Bring the boxed corners together and sew (see Techniques, page 37). Do this on both corners of the outer and both corners of the lining. Turn the bag through to the right side. Sew up the gap in the lining by hand or machine.

RESOURCES

STOCKISTS

SEWING MACHINES

Bernina
www.bernina.com

HABERDASHERY

John Lewis
For bag-making metalware, interfacings, general haberdashery, thread, template plastic, scissors and rotary cutting equipment
www.johnlewis.com

Dunelm
For quilt batting, threads, general supplies
www.dunelm-mill.com

Groves
For bag-making findings, general haberdashery, 505 quilt basting spray, cotton quilt battings, fusible, Sew Easy rulers and general cutting equipment
www.grovesltd.co.uk

Vliesofix
For interfacings, volume fleece, quilt batting, fusible foam, waist shaper, Decovil.
www.vliesoline.com

Bosal Foam and Fibre
For In R Form fusible foam and a range of stabilisers
www.bosalonline.com

Visage Textiles
For general haberdashery, Stuart Hillard Fabric Collections, cotton fabrics, quilt batting and Bosal products.
www.visagetextiles.com

FABRICS/BAG MAKING EQUIPMENT/ INTERFACINGS AND FOAM

Amazon
www.amazon.com

The Cotton Patch
www.cottonpatch.co.uk

Lady Sew and Sew
www.ladysewandsew.co.uk

The Bramblepatch
www.bramblepatchonline.com

Plush Addict
www.plushaddict.co.uk

Deanys Fabrics
www.deanysfabrics.co.uk

Makower UK
www.makoweruk.com

The Craft Cotton Company
www.craftcotton.com

ACKNOWLEDGEMENTS

I wrote "Bags for Life" in 2020 during the first lockdown, the most challenging year that I think most of us have ever faced. I could never have accomplished such a feat had it not been for an incredible amount of support from family and friends. Thank you to my wonderful husband, Charlie, whose unwavering belief in me is a constant source of strength. Thank you for your gentle words of encouragement, your positivity and your occasional modelling... you have always provided a shoulder when I needed it.

Thank you to my agent, Heather and also to Elly and Rob at HHB Agency for championing me and driving me forward with such kindness and love. I owe a huge debt of gratitude to my publisher, Pavilion, and to Helen, Sophie, Alice, Rachel, Emma and Kang who worked so hard to make this book such a thing of beauty.

I also relied very heavily on the support of friends and colleagues in the sewing and crafting industry to help me locate the materials and tools I needed when the shops were closed. A massive thank you to Nik and his wonderful team at The Cotton Patch and the fabulous team at Lady Sew and Sew headed up by dear friends Judy, Vanessa and John who helped me choose fabrics over the phone and whose ability to describe designs and colours are second to none! Thanks also to the incredible team at Vlieseline who sent interfacings and battings at incredible speed when I needed them most and my very special friends at The Craft Cotton Company who kept me topped up with Bosal products and fabrics when I just needed half a metre more!

To my wonderful friends, thank you from the bottom of my heart for your continued love, kindness and encouragement. In particular thank you Maxine, Amanda, Damian and Lisa, who helped me when I needed it most.